MW01705850

audience

www.worldaudience.org

audience

World Audience, Inc.

(www.worldaudience.org)

Issue # 3

December, 2006

New York

ISBN 978-1-934209-09-7

10-digit ISBN 1-934209-09-0

(ISSN and LOC numbers will begin in a 2007 issue.)

$11.99

World Audience (www.worldaudience.org) is a global consortium of artists and writers, producing *audience* and *The audience Review*. Please submit your stories, poems, paintings, and photography to: submissions@worldaudience.org; inquiries about being a reviewer: theatre@worldaudience.org. Thank you.

TABLE OF CONTENTS

Stories

Poetry

Plays

Interviews

Essays

THE FOLLOWING EXCERPT IS FROM *THE JESUS TAPES,* A NOVEL IN PROGRESS ALREADY CONTRACTED FOR PUBLICATION WITH SEVEN STORIES PRESS (http://www.sevenstories.com/) WHEN FINISHED. THIS PREVIEW IS OFFERED EXCLUSIVELY TO WORLD AUDIENCE, INC. AND MAY NOT TO BE REPRODUCED IN HARD COPY, OR POSTED ON ANY OTHER SITE WITHOUT THE EXPRESS WRITTEN PERMISSION OF THE AUTHOR.

The Jesus Tapes

by Calvery "Lee" Stringer

ii.

This was all before what happened in the laundry which is what I started telling you about in the first place; about what went down there and how that got me to thinking on what Baldwin said. It's only three of his books they got here that I found in the library. One was *Tell Me How Long The Train's Been Gone,* which it wasn't about no train, really, but about some famous actor who, right off from jump street when you open up the book, is having a heart attack and he starts thinking about his life--being that death's knocking on his door and all--about all the things he's done. About all the things he ain't done too. Thinking about what it all means.

I was like, *right on*, when I read it. Because that's the kind of shit a guy will be pondering, when you're in the joint. Really? It's damn near the same thing as dying, being locked down. Like, say you got a lady right? And you think you and her are all tight and shit. You're hitting the pussy real good. And being all helpful considerate and talking to her. Even listening to what she says which with woman is even better than sex to them sometimes. You doing all that, figuring doing all that you ain't got to worry about anyone else parking their car in your garage, if you get my drift. Yeah. Well, let me set you straight on that. Eight-nine months with you being on the lockdown and it will sure as hell cool that shit right down a lot sooner than you think. Word.

But I was talking about this book, which it was the second one of his books I read, really. The first one of his I checked out, the one that got me into reading the other two, is called *Go Tell It On The Mountain*, which if you want to know the truth, half the reason I picked it up is on account of I saw the movie on TV back when I was a kid. Me and my uncle Percy.

I got three uncles live right there in the hood, but I don't hardly see none of them except Percy. Percy's the only one out of all of them give me the time a day. You know, come by the house to see my moms--even though he's from my father's side of the family; take me to the corner for candy and shit. Percy was always ready to play with me, you know horse around and what not. Leastwise when I was real young and shit he did.

Whatever.

Really, I didn't even want to watch the movie all that tough being the thing was so lame. No action or anything. Just some preacher's son, moping around about not wanting to join the church which, according to his father, he was definitely going to do or else. But percy cut it on and wouldn't let me change the channel so I had to sit through it, which I didn't see the whole thing. I fell asleep about halfway. Next thing I knew I was in my pajamas in bed. It was just me and Percy and I still don't know how he got me out of my clothes and into bed all without me waking up. But he did it.

But even just seeing part of the movie, it gets me kind of curious when I come across the book sitting there on the shelf in the library. So I check it out and I go to my hole and start reading the thing and before you know it it's lights out and I fall asleep without pounding my hammer--thinking about tearing up a piece of ass which there ain't none of in this place. Not even conjugal visits like they have is some of those other places.

The thing is, with the book instead of the movie I mean, is you get all involved with the story more. Get inside of this kid's head--James his name was--more than just watching him on the screen, which you can't hardly see what he's thinking. I mean, reading the book, if you can stick with it through the boring shit, you kind of get to know this kid. And, you know what? He's a lot like me, this James boy. A lot like when I was a kid, leastwise. Which I had the same kind of thing about church he did, only not with my old man like him. Shit. My old man could care less about shit, which he don't live with us any more really since he went and got himself hooked on that pipe. All he care about is getting himself another rock of crack to hit up.

No with me it was my moms trying to push all that holy roller business on me. Don't get me wrong that I love her and all. I mean she's the one gone and brought me into this world, so push come to shove ... You only get one mother, know what I'm saying? Just that all that God stuff she be hitting me with all the time. Drove me straight out the house sometimes. Before my temper got the best of me and what not, I'd walk out. Can't be yelling and scraping with your mother, know what I'm saying?

It wasn't even that I had me all that big of a problem about God, per se. I mean I just figured on he's up there, all the wonders in the world and all. And heaven? Who knows? I never been all that tight with something I never seen, but, why not? But as for down here? In this lifetime? Well. I didn't see all that much connection, one thing to another, far as that goes. I mean take my mom, for example. Got three kids, one already in the grave and me on the lockdown. She no man to speak of, just a crack fiend for a husband which she got to keep an eye on her purse whenever he comes around. Not that there's all that much for the son of a bitch to steal, it being she's only got half a job which even then she got to sneak around to do it under the Welfare man's nose so she don't get cut off. And I ain't *never* seen her go out and buy a little something something for herself.

So when she comes on with all that moaning and groaning over Jesus, all that hand-clapping, foot-stomping, yes Lord, go-to-church-on-Sunday-and-twice-more-out-the-week business, all I kept thinking, but didn't say, out of respect for her being my moms and all, is, *What did it ever do for her?* No sir. I told myself, If it *is* there, some connection between what's up there and what's down here, well, life hadn't hardly bothered to show it to me.

This kid in the book, see, was the same way. Maybe not exactly like me. Maybe not calling the whole thing bullshit, but like he's got to follow his own heart, which is me all over too. I may not have a pot to piss in. I may not look like no movies star, not saying I'm ugly or anything. And I for damn sure ain't nobody's genius. But all that said, still nobody can tell me how to live I don't want to live that way. Word up.

Just like with me doing all this reading. I know they're all looking at me with their lip all turned up, wondering who the fuck I'm pretending to be. Don't make me no difference. Ain't about nobody going to love you here in the first place. I just put them on the no-never-mind. Even when it got around what the other James Baldwin book they got in here, *Giovanni's Room,* was about which to tell the truth I couldn't get into all that much when I read it on account of it being all about about some homo living in France and what it's like living with this other homo there who liked women too. Nobody actually come out to my face when it got around I was reading that. But all of us living all on top of each other, there ain't no secrets. I can tell some of them be wondering what's up.

So I read the book word for word, which I might of put it down otherwise, just because of that. But Really I don't know what was going through his mind, a famous writer like that, writing about that shit, except for maybe he was out to shock people so they'd be all talking about his book and whatnot. To tell the truth, when you get down to it it wasn't all that shocking no ways. Not it that way. I mean there wasn't a bunch of sucking dick or ass fucking or none of that in there. Far as I could make out, it was mostly about how down on himself the guy was for being a homo in the first place.

Okay, I'm going on and on about these books which the reason is they figure into what I'm trying to tell you about because it's on account of them I got switched to the job in the laundry, which is where, I already told you, what went down took place. See, one day the coach seen me with a book that ain't a school book--we have to go to classes here, it's *mandatory*--and he asks me what I'm reading and I show him the book and he looks at it and he says "Baldwin, huh?" and I tell him yeah, you hear of him? and he kind of shakes his head--trying to wrap his mind around me reading books when I don't have to, I figure, because Lord knows I don't give off that kind of impression.

"Yeah, I know him. Read that there booj myself" he says, still looking at me. Then he shakes his head again but with a halfways smile on his face this time and says, "You never know."

Coach is from Chicago. He was pretty big there once, coaching B-ball at one of them high schools a bunch of players made it all the way to the NBA come from. I don't know how he got up in here. Ugly, mean-looking som'bitch too which it's probably why they got him in here. Make you think twice about fucking with him. Got one of them big, nasty ole hook noses that's all dented in and wrinkled up between the eyes. Like someone bashed him one in the face with the back of a shovel or something. And you don't hardly never see him crack a smile, neither. They got maybe fifteen of us from D block in his class, which is for high school equivalency. You know, the three Rs and all. A little science and history in there too. Really, they just throw the whole shithouse at you hoping enough of it sticks maybe you squeak through the GED test enough to pass.

Anyway, from then on coach kind of took an interest in me--figuring I'm down with his whole bother which is being all educated and so forth--See what I mean about everybody trying to push their shit on you?--which I'm not saying I don't let him *think* I'm down with it. You got to play the player sometimes, you don't want him playing you. I put it to him how much I love to read and all, expand my mind, get knowledge, that kind of rap, but that after work detail I'm too tired to read all that much. I tell him this, see, to keep him from pushing a whole lot of other books on me I don't want to read. I mean the man's got to be fifty if he's a day. Got to be into some major corny ass shit he thinks is gold. So I keep running this on him and next thing you know, the Duty Captain that's what they call the guy who gives out the jobs here, I hear him telling me *T*runsdale, you got laundry. And I say laundry? And he says right back, Yeah, Laundry. You're on transport-which all this is is going around with a big basket on wheels, collecting all the dirty clothes and shit, then wheeling them back to the cells after they been cleaned. Pretty easy work, considering. Fucking coach. If I'd of knew he had that kind of pull I'd of played him big time, sure enough.

So now half the niggers in here hate my guts on account of that I got this cushy job so fast which they all wish they could of had. But hey, man. Don't blame me for living. The grave yard's full enough, know what I'm saying? Then, couple a weeks, a month maybe, I go down there and they got this new kid in there. A white boy, too. Skinny, choir boy looking motherfucker couldn't be more than eighteen--nineteen or in there, which you got to wonder what he done to get himself locked up. And get this; turns out he just got here last week and already he's down with the easy work, sorting. See, each con got him a nylon bag with his name on it for laundry and it goes in the machines like that, bag and all. And what the sort man does is separate the bags out by blocks and tiers, then I come along with the baskets and wheel the shit back to where it goes.

I can see why everyone in here is after my job. I mean it's easy and all, but the thing is you get to go all around the joint doing it and, come to find out ater just a few days at it, it's part of the underground courrier system they got here. You want something smuggled to your cell it's either the library cart or the laundry cart's going to get it there under the CO's noses. Sometimes the CO's is in on it too, you know which one to approach.

Talk about not liking a guy the minute you lay eyes on him. I don't know what it is, just something about this dude rubs me the wrong way so bad I can't no ways hardly stand the sight of him. I'm talking about hating this motherfucker. Hate at first sight, pure and simple. Word up.

Up Yours, Mate!

by Matthew Ward

"Up yours, mate!" The cabby gave me a very filthy-looking middle finger and roared up toward the centre of Gosford. He was a bit pissed off that I only had a fifty for a $10.00 trip; I had uttered something like: 'Yeah, well *that's* gotta hurt – y'can't get rid of those precious rednotes, can you, *hey* Gung-a-din...?', and so he gave me a handful of fives and coins, saluted me in *his* way and was gone.

Still, despite the cabby's shittiness, I felt as if I was everywhere all at once – in the daytime taking on this powerful persona. Just hang on and I'll tell you why.

Strangely enough, I had been to confession for the first time in 15 years, done my duty, all of my frustrations *Gone,* all of my fears, all my guilt *Splitsville,* taken away from me and I was free again. Religion could make me free, I told myself, when used in the right way. And have a chuckle, Mister Safe-Atheist, but I ain't gonna judge you. *I* was free and that was all I cared about.

And so I decided to celebrate my cleansing by flirting with another man's woman. As the Yanks say: As you do...

My confidence was overflowing. I was single again, my last lady had decided enough was enough and headed north to Cairns in her rustbucket Falcon, and for me there was no reason *not* to go out and have a good time. And there was no-one who could resist my charm. This was just how I felt.

The following day, I took a trip to Sydney, just to get away, clear my thoughts, maybe get lucky. Train. The trip was nothing special, just cows and trees, graffiti and signal boxes. It reminded me of a journey I did when I was 17 with a mate, Grant, the Saturday or Sunday (I cannot recall which day it was) when we went to Sydney and were horrified to see Manly get spanked by Norths at Brookvale Oval in what they in the press referred to as 'the local derby', and I remember it more because Grant and I were close friends and that it was the last I would see of him as he was moving to America to work. I had laughingly suggested he was going there to be a spy and he laughed back, but not too loud making me wonder if it was indeed true.

I was in my own version of Fritz Lang's *Metropolis*, Sydney, and I was in the mood for some crappy food so McDonald's was first on the list, the big one in George Street. I went there especially because the most recent ex- just uttered about was a fanatic Maccas hater. She went on and on about multi nationals taking over the world. Communist. She said all this while we wasted time waiting for our crispy crust at Pizza Hut. For me,

Maccas was a hit-out at her – at her and her stupid beliefs, and her boyfriend, the one she preferred over me. The one in Queensland. Never let a woman go on holiday on her own. Remember that and all will be well.

Anyway, I approached the counter feeling all cocky, all single and the gal who served made my heart beat a little bit faster. She was about 17, I guessed, blonde hair tied back under a blue-peaked cap. Name of Shelley. Earring in her nose – well, a stud not a ring for all of you picky cats out there, and when she served me she smiled, and not in that fake smile they are taught to smile in those Maccas training programmes – this was genuine, she liked what she saw, and when she smiled, I melted.

The accent was London, and *sweet girly* London at that, all innocent, all virginal like as gentle as Princess Di before the wedding and ensuing royal engagements... you remember, surely? She said: "Can I help you, sir?"

'Sir'? She had called me 'Sir'. I was touched. I ordered my burger, fries, Coke, gave her the money and as she gave me the change ("Have a nice day"), she dropped the coins in my hand and *slid* her hand along mine – my sudden inhale of the realisation of such a flirty move – her cheeky smile and my smile back, too.

Of course Shelley may not have been flirting , like maybe she flirted with *all* the male customers who looked half-decent to her and she might have been what we at school called a *prick-tease,* but then I didn't actually see it if it happened – from the way I saw it I was her bright ray of sunshine in another long day.

I found a spot near a window so I could gaze out at the people as they passed and all the women I gazed at looked as scrumptious to me as the hot, salty fries I gently crunched – the girls were all heavenly and when they passed they gave me that slow motion filmic gaze and smiled and some with long lashes tongued lips innocently as it was summer and hot outside, the morning sun streaked upon them from in between tall buildings – and I saw it all.

I had grabbed a copy of the Telegraph and read it, placed it on my left (these were copies bought by the place for the customers to read and they had red rubber stamp warnings of 'Do not remove if you know what's good for you' or something like that). And I fingered through the latest in domestic news (strikes, abductions, holdups, kittens rescued from pipes) and world (strikes, rebellions, bombings, Presidents touring Eastern Europe) and I picked the huge burger up in both hands and tore into it, dribbles of sauce and pickles spotting the paper tray mat advertising Kakadu. Coke with huge chunks of ice and sucked up with that *clok-clok* sound.

Across my way a couple sat down. Girl and guy. She looked 22, he was a bit older. Here's the thing: he is 5 foot 8, blonde hair in a stupid square cut with distinct fringe like a bad bob job and he's got daggy square glasses and his clothes are like button shirt in patterns like almost tartan but more pale in pastels and his trousers are cream baggy with brown belt and suede shoes. She's different: dark blouse with loose sleeves, skirt draping to her ankles with shoes, she has bangles on her ankles, her hair's dark brown and shortish, her face slim, and I think: 'What the fuck's she doing with him?' I thought: 'Hang on, could be her brother,' but then he reached over and kissed her cheek. He then seemed to be asking her what she wanted, then he left.

Now, I am not an expert on many things, but this I do know: women are much, much better at perving than men are. Men, it appears, seem to *want* to get caught - it's like asserting strength, our masculinity if you will. We also seem to forget what the woman looks like; yeah, okay, we recall they are pretty and have dark hair, say, and blue eyes, but the rest is a blur – at least this was the case with me. Women on the other hand seem to *not* want to get caught. I think with chicks it's gotta do with not wanting to be seen as easy or something, plus I read they have the ability to turn their head, catch a glimpse, then store that image to have a look at it when they want, forever!

So, then I felt the eyes upon me. I looked up to the dark-clad lass and she was going through her wallet. I went back to my eating. Then again that feeling of being watched and again like before I looked but flicked my eyes from the paper to the lass but she was not looking! This was driving me insane. I can hear you saying: yes but maybe she wasn't looking at me at all, and you know I thought this but was convinced; but how to trap her?

Meanwhile, the boyfriend came back with the food, placed a burger in front of her (even unwrapped it for her – what a guy!) and a shake as well, and when he sat down she thanked him with a peck on the cheek.

Me with the reading, sipping the Coke and once more the feeling! Then I had an idea: I continued reading and yawned. That's all, just yawned – worked one up from nowhere, waited 5 seconds and looked over to the girl. Hey presto! – she was yawning, holding a hand to her mouth. I kept looking and she looked to me and giggled. (You see, if you see someone yawning, you *have* to yawn, you have no choice – I read about it in a medical journal.)

Well, we exchanged knowing glances, flicked silently from one side of the place to the other. I gave her the gesture of 'Who's the guy?' and 'Is he with you?' and her 'I'm with *him* but sometimes wonder why' look. Our smile. She licked her lips, I licked mine. The boyfriend looked at the girl, then over at me (I could hear him): "What are you doing, Julia?"

The girl shook her head: "Nothing..."

Guy: "I saw you looking at him. Are you interested?"

Girl, shaking her head: "No, don't be so bloody stupid."

Guy: "So now I'm stupid, am I?"

Girl: "I didn't mean it *that* way..."

Guy: "Well, we'll see about this..."

The guy comes over to where I sat. I knew he was there but I kept eating and reading. He stood over me, his shadow on my paper.

Guy: "Hey!"

Me: "Yeah?"

Guy: "Keep your eyes offa my girl."

Me: "She's *your* girl?"

Guy: "Yes"

Me: "Do you have a receipt?"

Guy, tilting his head: "What?"

Me: "Do you have a receipt? You say she's *yours*, like a possession , man, so you should have proof of ownership; like, we're living in the *17th century*, dig?

The blonde dweeb thought about this, his face all red, then he snapped: "She's mine!"

Me, calmly: "You *said* that. What's your point?"

Guy: "My point, smartarse, is keep your eyes offa her!"

Me: "She's very pretty..."

Guy: "I *know* she's pretty, I know *that* - just *fuck off* and read yer paper!"

Me: "Attached?"

Guy: "What?"

Me: "Attached? Is she with anybody?"

Guy: "Yes! Me! Are you an idiot?"

Me: "You talking to me?"

Guy: "No, the guy over there" (points).

Me: "Oh, SAR-casm..."

Guy: "You're-making-me-ANGRY!"

I sat up straight, folded my arms and leered at him: "Look, mate, if I wanted to I could *have* her. She's been giving me the eye for half an hour and it is obvious she's only with you for convenience. You *buy* her things. You *upwrap* her food. You probably even open *doors* for her. You're-a-good-boy, Charlie-Brown. But I tell ya, if you keep up with this jealous shit you're gonna lose her.

Guy: You prick!"

Me: "'Prick', am I? Well, for that... In fact, mate, I *curse* your relationship and I would expect another 2 weeks or less; she'll run to another man. I can see it all, it's bound to happen..."

Guy (laughing): "Who, You?"

Me: "Not me, just anyone. Anyone but *you*. You're a dick, son."

He turned to the girl and said: "Come on, we're going!"

She shook her head, picked up her tray and came over, sat next to me and said: "Anything interesting in the news?"

Guy (tilting his head again, blinking his eyes rapidly): "Ummm, we're *finished*, Julia. Yeah this is the last time you do this to me! And you can expect your stuff out on the lawn when you get home, you bitch!"

And with that, he left.

I felt satisfied, yet for a while I felt guilty: I had driven these two apart.

She said to me: "I said: anything interesting in the news?"

Me: "Well, you know the deal: civil war, there's disease everywhere, yet love and peace in other lands.

Outside, I could hear a car locking up its brakes, then a hot blast of a horn. I looked up through the window to the street, and there was the yellow cab from Gosford; the cabby, smiling with his middle finger up to me again, his teeth black, yellow and grey, and above the noise of the traffic I could hear him roar: "I see you, mister Money-bags – Ha-ha! – Up yours, mate!"

Rubies on a Mossy Idol

by Hareendran Kallinkeel

Muthu watched as the man in front of him rocked, his wobbling potbelly undulating as bursts of his laughter rippled through the night air.

Muthu waited, bated breath and a calm face concealing the turmoil that boiled within. He could never understand the ways of tantrics. Sometimes they acted like lunatics, but they were men of wisdom. Equipped with the armors of Vedas and Mantras, armed with the knowledge gleaned from experience, they had the power to perform the rituals that brought any deity to their service. And they never went wrong. This one was no different.

The tantric stopped laughing and looked into Muthu's eyes. "You ignored my warnings, and went on as if you could take care of your life."

"I regret my follies," Muthu said. The twitch of a feeble muscle in his caved-in cheek left a bitter taste in his mouth. "I've suffered the consequences, and I'm in utter despair."

The tantric nodded. "I knew you'd come back to me. It was just a question of how long you'd take."

“Poverty has ruined my life. Destitution is sucking me in like quicksand,” Muthu said. “I don’t want riches. Just enough for my children to eat a decent meal.” He averted his eyes. “For me to have a good drink.”

“Only Mari Amman can save you from the clutches of poverty,” the tantric said, and sat back in rapt contemplation, running a hand along his flowing beard. Streaks of gray gleamed from the matted strands of his hair as pale moonlight cast dark shadows across his face.

Muthu waited for him to continue.

The tantric resumed after a while, glancing at Muthu’s eager face.

“But she needs blood. The younger the blood is, the more pleased she’ll be.” He moved closer to a bonfire that burned between them.

Rain clouds eclipsed the crescent, and shadows bobbed over the bonfire’s dancing flames as if grotesque images were prancing on the moon’s surface. An owl hooted on a tree near them. Its hollow voice echoed in Muthu’s ears with a sharp resonance. He gazed in its direction, and saw the dark silhouette of a hooked beak as leaves hid the rest of the predator’s body.

He envisioned a slippery head in its mouth, a writhing body hanging down, coiling and unwinding, lashing out a tail in the fury agony brought. Again. And again.

A shudder ran through Muthu's frail body as his bony fingers curled into tight fists. He had an ideal candidate in mind. She was the one who brought him to his doom. Her birth signaled a bad omen, and the tantric had warned him of imminent calamity. But he chose to ignore the tantric at his own peril and met the aftermath, unable to utter any protest. First, he'd lost his job, and then his property and livestock.

She would be the answer to his distress. When she was gone, his ill fate would disappear, too. Mari Amman would be pleased with her blood, and he'd be getting rid of her for good.

"Can I offer a pubescent girl?" he asked the tantric.

The fire burned with a new vigor as the tantric added more fuel to it. Hissing flames glazed his face with a fierce orange glow. He smiled, revealing tobacco-stained teeth, and sneaked a hand inside his dhoti, scratching his inner thigh.

"Ideal, I must say. The Goddess will be propitiated," the tantric said, picking at his matted gray hair with long-nailed fingers. "She'll shower you with wealth."

Flames danced in the tantric's bloodshot eyes, and Muthu felt a pang clutch at the walls of his stomach. "But isn't she the Goddess of the dark, the avenging angel?" he asked. A chilly gust lashed against his naked upper torso, and he stretched his arms over the flames. "Wouldn't she punish me for such a gruesome deed?"

The tantric laughed, and pulled his shawl tighter around his shoulders. "You're such a simple soul!" His thick eyebrows knotted, and wrinkles formed on his ash-smeared forehead. "You're granting holy deliverance to a sinful soul. Those sacrificed to the gods would be reborn as blessed ones. This life is her cursed call; the next will be her reparation."

Muthu watched the burning twigs. "It's known that victims of untimely death end up in hell."

"For one who dies for the Goddess, it's different. So is it for the one who facilitates such a death." The tantric picked up another handful of kindling and threw it on the fire. Tiny sparkles erupted like a cluster of fireflies. "Mari Amman gleans life from death for those who favor her." He bowed his head, joined his palms together in salutation, and touched his forehead where his eyebrows met. "Her blessings will lift you up to the stars."

Muthu looked up at the dark sky devoid of stars, and crossed his arms against his chest. The wind picked up momentum, and its icy tongue licked off the warmth the bonfire left on his skin.

"Tomorrow is full moon. Bring her here after midnight," the tantric said. "There are certain rituals that I should perform before the sacrifice."

"Will everything be all right?" Muthu asked.

"Perfectly." The tantric stood up. "Prosperity is in your fate. You've realized your karma. But make sure you don't let the cat out of the bag."

Muthu stood up and nodded.

* * *

Muthu hated the black cat. It was a bad omen, like his daughter.

The ugly feline's presence always unsettled his nerves. It had this weird habit of sneaking between his daughter's legs, pushing its body against her ankle and walking around her, while its tail brushed her calves in what seemed like tantalizing strokes. She'd squeeze her half-skirt's hem between her thighs, squat on her haunches, lift up the cat and start petting it. The cat would graze its face against her chest and begin purring.

It stopped the noise and activities when Muthu appeared on the scene, and stared at him with eyes glowing like emeralds, tail whipping viciously, ears pricked and rotating as if tuning to some threat perception, whiskers pitched forward.

Today, when he climbed the stone steps and entered the verandah, he heard a sound akin to a hiss. His first notion was that of a serpent, but then a deep growl followed. He noticed the cat's dark silhouette moving towards him in a prancing, sideways motion.

It grew in size with each step toward him, claws emerging from its paws like shining sickles.

Cursing, Muthu ran towards his hut's entrance, thrust the door open and, once inside, slammed it shut with all his strength. Some considered cats as animals that brought prosperity. Like Garuda, the Divine Eagle, was thought to be Vishnu's carrier, felines were considered as carriers of Durga, another form of Mari Amman. But Muthu doubted these theories. He hated cats; they were a menacing presence.

After a dinner of boiled tapioca and dried sardine roasted in palm oil, he sat with his wife, Kali, on a mat on the floor of their only bedroom, and discussed his plans. Despite the tantric's warning, he deemed it fit to divulge his intentions to his wife. There was no way he could hide things from her. And her involvement would only enhance his chances of escaping the law, if ever anybody got suspicious. He knew police in this remote village wouldn't take any notice of a missing girl, unless there was a complaint and someone keen enough to prod them with steady follow-ups. But in any case, one was prudent not to take chances.

"Nobody can change destinies," Kali said. "Neither your tantric nor his Goddess. You should rather toil harder for prosperity."

"I work hard in the master's estate." Muthu glanced at his children huddled in a corner, a patched blanket barely covering them, and then his eyes bored into hers. "But I hardly earn enough to support a full stomach for us all. Before she arrived, we were well off. It's a pity her birth signaled such misery, and we had to lose everything."

"Don't blame your child for your follies." Kali stared out into the dark night through the single window. "You lost your job because you couldn't stand up to your responsibilities. The property, because you'd been reckless." She turned her face towards him; swept teardrops welling in her eyes with the back of a hand. "Stop spending on arrack, and your get-rich-quick schemes. We'll have enough to fill our stomachs."

Muthu averted his eyes from her face. He had been spending most of his earnings on animal sacrifices and related pujas and rituals. He had even borrowed hefty sums from moneylenders to defray the expenses, and a good chunk of his wages went to paying the interest. But ultimately, it was going to pay back. He would receive the blessings of the deities and become rich. This last effort was going to change his destiny forever. The tantric had guaranteed that.

He lighted a beedi, and took a deep drag. "I don't want my fate sealed forever, to suck on the bitterness of a beedi." He grimaced, taking another pull. "I should be able to afford cigarettes instead of beedi, and whisky rather than arrack."

Muthu heard Kali cough. She always did when he lighted a beedi. The smell made her wheeze; her lungs were allergic.

He looked at her pockmarked face. As a teenager, she had suffered from chicken pox. That was before he'd married her. Kali had told him she was taken to a Mari Amman temple in the city, where she was laid on a stretcher made of bamboo sticks and coconut fronds and carried around the shrine, like the dead were transported to their grave, her relatives following.

"I don't know whether it was something in the coconut fronds, or the herbs, spices and ghee incinerated in the sacrificial pit during the prayers, or the power of the deity," she had said. "But everybody believed it was the latter. So, I did too."

He took a final drag of the beedi and threw it out the door. "In a couple of years she'll be sixteen," Muthu said, indicating his eldest daughter. "How do you think we'll manage the dowry for her marriage?"

Kali's frail body rocked in another bout of coughing.

"It's the fault of your cursed womb; five girls in a row!" Muthu said, grinding his teeth. "Not a single boy to fetch us some dowry."

"They didn't just sprout in my womb." The pitch of Kali's voice rose. "Who spawned the seeds? And poverty is no excuse for any drastic step."

"Philosophy is for the masters, don't you understand? You and I need to do away with the gnawing in our stomachs. Think about the kind of money that could buy us enough food," Muthu said, searching his pocket for another beedi, "and necessary comforts."

"I know your intention." Kali heaved a sigh. "And I know nothing justifies it. Men can't change their destiny. I believe in God's ways."

"Whatever I do is for our common good." Muthu cast a threatening glance at his wife. "And if you try meddling with my plans, I've no option but to kill you all, and then myself. Death is far better than this wretched life."

He saw embers burn in Kali's eyes, and remembered Mari Amman's idol lying in a cluster of bushes behind the tantric's hut. Moss had covered most of the stone, except the eyes that shone like emeralds…

He knew of Mari Amman's powers. She was the Swayambhoo; she originated from the earth's womb; no sculptor had to carve out her figure from stone. She became the idol, and a reality, on her own.

He fell silent.

* * *

The next day, Muthu sat in the verandah, smoking beedi after beedi, waiting for others to sleep. He did the right thing by not telling his wife when he planned to execute his scheme. She wouldn't expect him to go about it so soon.

He sneaked into the bedroom and heard Kali snore. The situation quite fitted his purpose. His eldest daughter was sleeping on the far side where he wouldn't have any problem holding the herb to her nose for a while. The tantric had told him it would render her unconscious for about an hour; enough time for him to smuggle her out to the destination.

The cat was asleep, snuggled close to her feet, purring in contentment. It was the only creature in the family that bore no manifestation of poverty. Sturdy and furry, it gave the impression of a well-fed feline. Obviously, the larger share of his daughter's meager food went to the cat.

Muthu carefully inched his hand towards the animal, grabbed at the skin on the back of its neck, and lifted it. The feline shuddered once, but did not move, and hung from his hand in the fetal position. He had learned the trick well. Held that way, the cat seldom had a chance of attacking.

With his other hand, he opened a gunny bag he carried, put the cat inside and, in a sweeping motion, tied its mouth, and made for the door. The cat jumped hither-thither and started growling as he placed it beside a tree outside and tucked the loose end beneath a large stone.

Muthu made his way back with silent steps, like a stalking feline.

* * *

Muthu sat warming his hands over the bonfire's flames. The acrid scent of burning wood wafted into his nostrils.

"The rituals will take about an hour. Got to prepare her; sprinkle her body with holy water and get her to recite some mantras," the tantric said, handing him a beedi. "When the rituals are over, I'll call out for you. You can then enter the hut and come to the yard through its back door. We'll be there."

The tantric left.

Muthu lit the beedi. It smelled and tasted different. Musky, its smoke felt sweet against his palate. This should be ganja, what some of his co-workers had boasted would take him to the thresholds of heaven.

After several pulls, he felt high, floating on the wings of the curling fog that shrouded the atmosphere like a haze, with lightness in his limbs, dryness in his mouth. He felt a glaze of gray veil his eyes, a soothing cover, like the comfort the master's glasses offered in the sun.

Where was the owl, and why didn't it hoot now? Muthu looked around into the darkness. Pods of cotton burst in the night sky in a staccato of popping sounds. White, fluffy cotton floated in the air like shreds of clouds.

At his side, the gunny bag convulsed like a woman in throes of labor.

Muthu jumped to his feet and approached the shaking figure. Kali, why are you lying on the ground? Our son must enter this world from an appropriate place, don't you think so?

Before his veiled eyes, the mass twisted in another spasm. The guttural growl felt like a woman's shrieks in his ears. He nodded in realization.

"Deliver me a male child," Muthu said. "One that portends a good omen."

"Did you sow the appropriate seed?"

Muthu looked around. No, Kali was fast asleep back at home.

More pods broke. The air filled with shreds of clouds. They sailed across and through the flames.

Muthu sniffed. Clouds don't burn.

The gunny bag twisted spasmodically again.

"Push," Muthu said in an excited voice. "Deliver me a lucky son."

The bag rocked in a series of spasms.

"Push harder." Muthu took another deep pull at the beedi.

The tip of a head appeared, struggling to squeeze through the tiny opening.

"What beautiful hair," Muthu said.

The head emerged.

"Why such an ugly baby?" Muthu asked, gazing at it. "But the color doesn't matter. No, it doesn't. He will be my lucky star."

Muthu approached as the body started coming out. Hands first, and finally the legs. He knelt to pick up the baby and stopped frozen as the cat growled, back arched like a taut bow, fur bristled, whiskers quivering, and fangs bared. It struck, lashing out with a paw. He felt the seething pain as claws tore at the back of his hand.

The cat fled into the hut, its strident cries splitting the silent night.

Muthu then heard a wail, shrill and piercing, and tried to stand up. The ground turned into a swamp, and pulled at his feet. He sat down. The ground gave in. He stood up. It revolved.

Another wail. It sounded like it came from inside his head. A sharp cry...it ricocheted against his eardrums, reverberated in his ears, and boomed within his skull. He slumped back to the ground.

His daughter was supposed to recite mantras; why would she cry?

And how did the bonfire burn so vigorously on sodden earth? Must be a miracle of the Mari Amman. The deity did have enormous powers!

Muthu stood up again, and walked towards the hut. Mud sucked at his legs as he waded through the swamp. The slush gurgled. He heard a yell. This time he was sure that it was not from inside his head. Somebody had shouted something. He heard the sounds, not the words. A sudden chill sliced through his body.

The ground hardened. Muthu ran into the hut.

* * *

A shrill wail made the cat pause. Paws firmly on the ground, claws extended, it gazed ahead, neck stretched, as if orienting itself to the darkness, and smelled a familiar scent. The girl was on the mat, flailing her limbs to ward off some evil. Walking stealthily towards her, it noticed the figure atop her, pinning her down and clawing at her chest.

Its eyes, glowing like emeralds in the murky night, dilated fully to take in the spectacle. Back arched, ears flattened against a silky mane, and black fur along its spine bristling, the feline's tail stiffened in a downward curve and the tip flicked steadily.

The cat released its fury in a piercing growl.

The tantric raised his hip, holding his organ with one hand, ready for insertion, when the cat pounced between his raised thighs, sank its fangs into his balls and clung there, forepaws dangling, hind legs drawn together in fetal position, like an enormous scrotum swollen by hydrocele. Its raised hackles fell back in harmony, but it wouldn't let loose its clutch on the testicles. The tantric roared, running in circles, scared to stretch his hand to his groin.

***

The girl lay on a mat, on a white cloth, with a clutter of rubies in her lap shining in the bright moonlight. Muthu ran toward her, grabbed fistfuls from between her legs, and felt a sticky wetness in his hands.

A rasping cry, like that of animals he has seen sacrificed to appease the deities, emanated from behind the hut. Muthu ran out.

Mari Amman stood, a butcher's knife raised in her hand. The tantric's body, lying tangled in the bushes, twitched. Blood from his truncated neck sprinkled onto the black idol. Mari Amman laughed, sweat trickling down her pockmarked face.

"Rubies! See--" Muthu opened his palms.

Mari Amman looked at his hand daubed in scarlet, and nodded.

"Rubies aren't as precious..." She wheezed.

Muthu stared into her eyes.

"...as avenging a daughter's death." She raised the blood-dripping knife.

Muthu squeezed his eyes shut against the fierce glow in her eyes.

* * *

The feline watched, hair flat against its back, upraised tail twitching in anticipation, as Muthu's rubies splattered on Mari Amman's black idol.

Grandiose Justice

by Ernest Dempsey

The accused rat was brought in chains before the jury and the judge. The authorized investigator sat behind the fence opposite the Accused's dock. The prosecutor settled before his table, throwing an arrogant glance at the Accused that stood indifferent and thoughtful. The judge smoothed his peruke with his hands before banging the table with the hammer. The proceeding commenced as the judge addressed the prosecutor.

Judge: Mr. Prosecutor, what charges do you bring against the Accused?

Prosecutor (standing up and coming forward): Your Honor, the Accused, as you see him in the dock, has a long list of offenses on his part ranging from violation of personal space to attempted murder. And as you preside over this session Mi Lord, I strongly urge the court to put the threatening thing to maximum punishment.

Judge: What do you say to this Mr. Accused?

Accused: Mi Lord, it's an honor for me to be given a chance to defend myself. I'll speak for myself if you allow me sir.

Judge: Oh well, it's good you can speak for yourself. Mr. Prosecutor would you please read out the charges against the Accused?

Prosecutor: Yes sir, I most certainly will. (Taking a set of papers out of his file he reads aloud) First of all the Accused is convicted of causing utter disturbance of varying sort among the inhabitants of Baker Mansion and the annex. Rushing around the corners while little children are around, making noise when it's bedtime, and waking people by rustling in bags and clothes, and more indirectly but intensely it plays havoc on people's peace by kicking up its arch enemy, the cats. More than eighteen people are living in anguish due to this disturbing conduct of the Accused.

Judge (looking at the Accused): How do you clear yourself of this?

Accused: Mi Lord, the charges of disturbance against me are nothing more than mere faulty daylights of the inhabitants of the said mansion.

Judge: What do you mean?

Accused: Just imagine yourself walking into a neighborhood to collect your food for yourself and your family. Your neighbors get conscious of you and rise to kill you for what you are doing. Who is to be regarded as insane? You or the neighbors?

Judge: My goddamned neighbors.

Accused: Same is the case here, Mi Lord. These men are after my life for fetching food for my poor and helpless children. Do I deserve death on account of making minor disturbances, which were not even made deliberately?

Judge: By no means fellow! The Accused is not guilty (bangs the table with the hammer).

Prosecutor: Won't you put an ear to his felonies that haven't been stated yet, Mi Lord?

Judge: You can proceed.

Prosecutor: Thank you Mi Lord! You were just taken in by the innocent appearance of one of the most horrible of things that have always posed a threat to humanity.

Accused: Oh! I am shocked to hear that. Would you make your point precisely?

Prosecutor: Mi Lord, waking up sleeping people isn't that trivial, as it seems in the first instance. Repeatedly waking up prematurely can build up nervous strain over time and this may well lead to accidents, suicides, and even murders. Would you let that go too, sir?

Accused: As far as I know, the inhabitants of the said mansion are woken up mostly by thunderstorms, earthquakes, and above all by telephone bells. Shouldn't you charge them with offense, Mr. Lawyer?

Prosecutor: What rubbish! Things you mention are all inanimate. How can we punish these?

Accused: Which seems to imply that you want to punish me simply because I am living and I can feel the pain.

Prosecutor: Thunderstorms and earthquakes are natural phenomena. They can't be stopped.

Accused: Very well sir. Am I not natural? My instinct for food is as natural as an earthquake. Just tell me how to stop it?

Prosecutor: You should have learned some manners of satisfying it.

Accused: We are not allowed to sit among your young ones to whom manners are taught neither can we get admitted to your schools, academies, nor to universities. How can we learn manners?

Prosecutor: Mi Lord, the Accused is going absurd. He is the cause of disturbance and he must be punished.

Judge (groaning): Well, do you have more to forward for conviction?

Prosecutor: Of course I have Sir! The Accused has caused accidents of serious nature at least five times in two months, involving children of the mansion. First, he frightened young Martha on the stairs, causing her to fall down and break her front teeth. Secondly, the horrid thing ran on the table before little Miles who choked almost to death by this. Third, poor little Fiona developed an incurable phobia and went insomniac when she found the brown devil on her shoulder in her bed. Fourth, the freak ate away the covering of Dr. Bones' room's electric wire and his young nephew Dave spent a week in the hospital on account of getting electrocuted with it. And finally, the accused devoured the porridge made for baby Sam and bit the child's finger which made him fright and fall down the bed to be hospitalized for ten days. Isn't all this a horrible account of his felonies?

Judge: It really sounds like that. Do you have anything to say to this?

Accused: Mi Lord, the learned gentleman has battered my self-respect by using words like 'horrid thing', 'devil', and 'freak'. Anyhow, all I can say to his charges, as posed against me, is that the said children hurt themselves because of the irrational fear put in their heads by their elder ones. Master Dave's case was just an accident and accidents do happen with no one rightly to blame for. Baby Sam held me and tried to pull my tail out. I bit desperately to save my life. The rest of the cases are the direct consequence of all sorts of horrible things that people tell their children against us.

Judge: You mean to say you didn't fright those children.

Accused: I mean to say I am not the root cause of their fright. They don't fright from dogs, cats, sheep, and many other of those more powerful and stronger creatures than I am. Then why me? What solid grounds do and can anyone have on which to base one's label of 'frightful me'?

Prosecutor: Your Honor, this is nothing else but poppycock. By questioning common sense matters the Accused is trying to baffle the court, only to get away with all that.

Judge (grunting): Well, I see. Is that all you have to bring against the Accused?

Prosecutor: No, Your Honor. My clincher is yet to come. Since we are short of time, I've to come to the point laconically. You must be familiar with 'plague' Mi Lord.

Judge (startling): What? For heaven's sake! Are you talking of that deadly, killing disease of rats?

Prosecutor: I am talking of the same Sir. Plague is a synonym of 'death' and the Accused is one of the kinds that impart this death to me, to you and to others to our kind. The Accused is a potential killer. One lapse of ours in his treatment and the whole city will be at stake. I hope you remember the tragic fate of London in this regard.

Judge (glowering at the Accused): Don't tell me scoundrel that you can vindicate your innocence in the face of this!

Accused: If my respectable prosecutor knows at least as little as a junior high school kid, he must acknowledge my innocence by the fact that fleas are the things imparting plague to men, and by ridding them off, men can save themselves. Besides, not all rats are carriers of plague. Furthermore, most of the scientific, particularly medical, research uses us for preparing all kinds of health stuff: the chemicals; the vaccines; the antibiotics; and all that. Millions of cancer patients are living rather pain-free lives because men infect us with deadly viruses. And they do this without fleas or mosquitoes. So tell me Mi Lord who pays it all, you or we?

Judge: This does not make any shit of a sense. You are the root cause of the killer plague. There's no denying it.

Prosecutor: Mi Lord, the wicked rascal is temporizing in order to prolong his noxious existence. I strongly urge you to condemn this threat to its fate so as to minimize the risk of its inflicting any calamity on us.

Accused: Temporizing? You don't mean to say it's over now, do you?

Judge: The evidences filed against you clearly prove you a horrible threat to humanity. You are sentenced to death with in twenty-four hours of the dismissal of this court. With this done, I declare the case dismissed here. (The judge bangs the table with the hammer. The prosecutor grins victoriously at the Accused and then looks back at the investigator.)

Two days later the widow of the Accused found a piece of paper enclosed in an envelope carrying the court's stamp and address. It was from her late husband, carrying his last words that he had written before his death. She read with a grieved heart: 'My sweet little wife, I'm going to leave you forever in a few minutes. They're going to kill me. Kiss my little kids for me one last time and tell them I died innocent. And yes, as soon as you read my words, take the children and get out of that house immediately. Make your way to the wild with our kids. It's much safer there than living among humans. Please take care that Lolibo brushes his teeth regularly. I do not want him to stink like the prosecutor. My case reveals to me that the meaning of reason and evidence, as acceptable these days, is far from what we have known it to be this far. Hire a human tutor for Melioba to equip her with fallacious logic, just in case the tragedy somehow strikes again. I hope you'll live peacefully after all.'

With love,

Rino

The Design

by Jean Russell

A silver-haired woman in a navy blue suit handed me the book. She smelled like face powder and old roses.

"I'll leave you alone while you look through this," she said.

"What do you want me to do?" I asked.

"Just look through it to see what you like. For the design, you know. Just take your time, dear. I'll be right back."

"I've never done this before," I complained, but she had closed the door quietly behind her.

I sat alone in a room that was decorated to look like someone's cozy den but the phony books and fake hanging plants reminded me where I really was. I wanted to leave.

Instead, I leafed through a few pages. There were colored pictures on every page: flowers, animals, religious symbols, and other illustrations, each with a number next to it like in a catalog. While I thumbed through it with my shaky hand, I felt pulled toward the "Musical" section. My hand stopped automatically at the picture of a guitar. My vision blurred for a moment. That's when I saw the face on the page, not much bigger than my thumb, right next to the guitar. I blinked a couple of times but he was still there. His brown eyes, so much like mine, crinkled at the corners when he told me, "Pick the guitar."

The lady returned with a long form in her hand. Obviously, she hadn't heard his voice. I rubbed my eyes. I had not worn makeup for several days.

"Now then," she said as she sat down across from me, "I have his complete name here. Is this correct?"

She pushed the form toward me. I glanced at it and shoved it back across the desk to her. "Yes," I answered, "it's correct."

"Now," she said, "have you selected something for our design?"

Not 'our' design, I wanted to tell her, I'm the one doing this but I said nothing. My hands shook as I leafed through the book, then flipped back to the guitar. There was my brother's face next to it again, smiling at me. "Take it easy," he whispered, "and pick the guitar."

"I want the guitar," I told her.

"All right, that's nice, dear. The guitar will go in the upper left corner. The name, of course, the full name, will go in the center. Now, what would you like to have in the other top corner?" She seemed to occasionally look over my shoulder out the window. I guessed it must be a boring job for her, to do this over and over all day long. She was very patient while she waited for me to answer.

"Can I get you some coffee or tea?"

I shook my head. She pushed the Kleenex box a little closer to me.

"Miss? In the other corner? Would you like something up there?"

Lady, I thought, I don't know what I want in the corner. I don't know anything but that I want to get out of here. But I had a job to do and I was determined to do it. There was no one else who could.

Absentmindedly, I turned the pages of the book. Whenever I stopped, I saw my brother's face looking at me, his brown hair that dipped like wings over each eye, and his brown mustache that would never turn gray. I looked up at the lady to see if she noticed him, but she was staring at me with perky blue eyes.

"Honey, I know this is difficult. Let me help you." She turned the pages very slowly, allowing me time to study each picture. "Do you like any of these?" She pointed to an angel with a harp.

"Nah," my brother said from the page, "keep goin'."

I looked at the angel and shook my head, even though I'm fond of angels myself. It was what I would've picked for myself to be carved into stone. But this design wasn't for me.

About a hundred pages later, in a different section called "Nature," there was a picture of a pine cone. My brother's face was on the page next to it. He said, "Pick the pine cone." I remembered when we went camping one time and he picked them off the trees to take home. So I told the lady I wanted the pine cone.

"Are you sure?" she asked. "No one ever picked that before. I don't remember that ever being selected."

"But it's part of the design," I told her. She patted me kindly on the arm, saying in a low voice, "Fine, dear, fine."

I took a deep breath while she wrote the number connected with the pine cone on her form. She held on to my arm for a second, telling me, "Now then, we're almost finished. All I need to do is confirm the dates with you. The birth date is September 15, 1958, correct?"

I nodded, wishing I could do anything but sit in this room with this woman making this design. But I couldn't stop now. It was almost finished.

She pushed the form at me again. There was a rectangular section of it where she had drawn in what I had selected so far. The name across the center, the guitar in the upper left corner and the pine cone in the upper right corner. The birth date was beneath my brother's name, followed by a dash and a blank space.

I had to look away from her and the form. There was a fake Renoir painting next to her on the wall - the one with the young woman holding a gray kitten. Only now they had company. My brother's face looked out at me from the corner of the painting. He looked sad now, as if he felt sorry for me. The whole painting blurred, then appeared to melt and drip down the wall, but his face was clear and began to multiply until it covered the walls of the room like some incredible, personalized wallpaper. His face was everywhere.

But, finally, I was able to speak and my vision returned to normal. "The date you want is November 9," I said, "Six days ago."

She handed me a lavender tissue as I stood up to leave. I was grateful. "Yes, dear," she said, "I'm sure he would like it. Don't you think so?"

I fumbled around with my car keys. She had been kind to me. I turned back before leaving the cemetery office. "I know he would," I told her, "He designed it."

Girl Sitting in Front of Unfinished Wall

by Mary C. O'Malley

Violet Heyman
Odilon Redon 1840-1916

She is almost part of the unfinished wall
her pastel dress complements the light
colors of spring flowers. Hyacinth Blues
and pink intermix with green and white.

She is almost part of the unfinished wall
sitting in a chair surrounded by gray space
which itself creates an outline, a shadow
or halo encircling her young female life.

She is almost a part of the unfinished wall
the wall becomes her, the left high corner
spilling out flora like an April cornucopia
an overflow and expectation of young life.

She is almost part of the unfinished wall.
The stiff side profile with brown hair
flowing down the back of her green dress
unknown to us who view her.

She is almost part of the unfinished wall
seen in the first bloom of visual experience
or is it a triad of painted layers the faint
blur of paint a scrim of unknowingness.

She is almost part of the unfinished wall.
This girl named Violet, the namesake
of another spring flower. She herself
a flower innocent of life and decay.

The Sheriff

by Mila Strictzer

Kid Mila rode into town
It was early
They saw him coming,
And kept firing at him;
But Kid Mila outsmarted 'em all,
Firing back with his six guns –
He won.
The sheriff and the lawmen
Were long gone from the dusty town,
And there was nothing; but
Lawlessness

Well.

Kid Mila, right away,
Fired up the place
And went in the bar
Calling out for Whiskey
Double
The barkeep served him proper
Kid Mila drank the glass,
Slammed it on the bar;
Then, he saw an old man,
Drinking at the other end of the bar;
So, Kid Mila said to him,
"Hey, old man,
what the hell's wrong with this place?"
The old man said, "I'm afraid
everything has been dead here
for over forty years."
"That long? –
(There was a pause.)

I'm a poet!" Kid Mila said.

"Longer," the old man replied.

Well,
Kid Mila finished his drink
And rode out to camp,
Got himself a gal
By name o Lady Persephone,
A few drinking buddies,
A second-hand computer,
A third-rate job –
And sometimes no job,
And a box –
Became a regular
At the low-down bars
The town began
To get wise to Kid Mila
Every time the townsfolk got lazy –
Well, Kid Mila,
He'd start shooting up the place
Well,
One day,
Kid Mila swung out 'a the bar,
Stumbling,
After drinking all night
It was daylight,
When the town crier
Came running up, and said,
"Kid Mila! They done stolt
your horse 'an both 'a your mules,
shot your dog plum dead;
plus, your gal's – well, she's with the perpetrator(s)."
"They shot my dog?"
"Yep."

"Don't these townsfolk have a strand of decency?
"Nope."
"They'll pay for shooting my dog."
"Whatcha gonna do, Kid Mila?"
Kid Mila said,
"It's a sad town ain't got no poets, brother.
It's a sad town.
But, the world's done gone global,
and I don't need to hang around here anymore
to prefect my craft; or, for much of anything,
for that matter.
I'm tired of it, and I'm leaving."
"So, you leaving, Kid Mila?
Huh?" The town crier whined.
"Yes, I am going down to Central America,
and I ain't coming back.
The women are prettier, dance better;
And, a poet can write his words in peace,
without them being stolen."
"Bye, Kid Mila."

But,
As Kid Mila was walking away,
The town crier said,
"I guess Vonnegut was right 'bout you."
"What?"
"Mr. Kurt Vonnegut – he's from parts back east,
and he said you're the running kind
'narry staying in one place for too long,
'cause you get mad and pout off like a baby –
he said watch out for you.
that's what Vonnegut said about you."
Kid Mila said,
"Well, you tell Mr. Vonnegut
I will *keep* running too –
until I get it right;

and, then we'll see what happens."

So Kid Mila walked into the sunset,
And the desert,
Because he did not have a horse
Anymore,
Or money for a new horse
After about four miles of tired walking,
Kid Mila turned around,
And went back to the low-down bar.

The Perfect Lawn

by Doug Holder

Far from Boston

I will neuter it.

I will

mow that plot

before the plot thickens,

cut all the intrusive

outside of the box

gay blades-

In my narrow mind

I picture a broad lawn

a perfect rectangle

where I draw the line

with the demarcation of lime--

no random weed

or itinerant seed

will drop

will mix

will be felt

on my flawless

green pelt

Interior Design

by Michele Harvey

Mother visited my home in South Florida for the first time.
It was a steamy and disorienting afternoon.
She was still inside.
I turned the front door key, squinting from the sunlight
and with disbelieving eyes, entered someone else's house.

The long rectangular, wooden shelf
with the wicker top and fitted glass panels
lined with the brass bell, Japanese doll and gold serving platter
was missing from the living room. The blue leather sofa had been
pushed into the center of the room; it's silhouette remained against
the empty white wall where it sat for the past six years.

"Honey, doesn't this look more inviting," mother asked, locking us
in old identity. She echoed words used when I was eight years old
and she rearranged my dollhouse furniture.
The lamp on the end table was unplugged and shoved into a closet.
Mother is ignorant of more than feng shui. She didn't clean the house.

Without words, I sped around like a freak on speed, reshuffling
furniture.
Who are you, I thought. What was I thinking when I invited you back
into my world?
I rearranged the interior of mother's suitcase
and told her to stay at a motel.

Loneliness On A Cabin Cruiser

by Joyce Andrea Rothenberg

Down here with all of you
on the lower deck
Brains immersed in jargon

Up to the higher deck all alone
No - I was all alone before

How strong
  euphoric
  brave
    I feel

What is happening
Why are you leaving me

Oh No -It's one of you
from the lower deck
taking me back to
          loneliness on a cabin cruiser.

Love is my Voice

by Mel Waldman

I will not speak today. Love is my voice.

Don't vanish, my darling,
My mind cries secretly
Across the
Void
Of
Drifting Forests, Raging Smoke,
In the sky.

The fires…!
Of such things, I can not speak.

We say goodbye (on a cell phone),
As we
Intersect
&
Intertwine
&
Break away,
Silently,
Alone!

Tower 1 falls!
Farewell, my love.
But not before
Our Spirits cling,
&
Uncanny union carries
Invisible pieces,
Of our smoky lips,

Oval fires
Of
Love
Across the galaxy!

Trapped in Tower 2,
I am.
Enclosed, but
Nestled within your love.
Our love.

Can you see it?
The beginning of life!
Created by eerie endings-
That connect-nothing!

Can you see it?
Charging toward the Void,
Yet unifying all,
Bereft.

Of such things, I refuse to speak.
And what I mention, is unknowable.

(Burnt flesh, metal, flesh-metal,
The misty, ghostly sounds;
The scent of white, metallic dusty Death;
The clatter, rattle, and roar
Of this fierce fire that
Chases
Vanishing
Souls
Far away-
Today.)

Can you hear a mystical call-

The cry of the shofar?

(And the light of holiness
Brushing the anguished/angelic
Faces of Abraham and Isaac?)

On this unholy, holy day,
As we pray,
We who are left, or leaving,
Vanish!

&
Across the
Void
Of
Drifting Forests, Raging Smoke,
In the sky,

A ram's horn
Shrieks
Sorrow/Salvation
On
A
White birch tree
Bending
Toward
The Heavens…

Tower 2 falls!
A woman's voice whispers: "I love you."

It travels far across the invisible universe.
And finds me-in a different place.

But of such things, I need not speak. Love is my voice.

Charlie's Oyster

by Edward L. Betz Jr.

(Story by Edward and Donna Betz)

SCENE 1

Lights bump up downstage. 1972, backstage of a college theater, CHARLIE FAUCHEUX and JOHN GOODMAN, both in their early 20's, are play boxing. John, un-athletic, isn't enjoying himself.

JOHN: I'm not complaining, it's just my size. The only way I'd get to play a lead is if I broke your nose, then I'd get to go on.

CHARLIE: Brando broke his nose and went on anyway.

JOHN: There ya go. (Beat) My luck. (Beat) No, man, you were great yesterday. You were Brando.

CHARLIE: Thanks.

TAS WALKER, early 20's, walks up to them, eating peanuts. Her focus is on Charlie. John watches her every move as he continues with Charlie, who gets aggravated that John's attention is elsewhere.

TAS (to Charlie): Stanley Kawouski, are you going to stop playing around and run lines with me?

Charlie stops and turns to her and sees the peanuts in her hand and draws back.

CHARLIE: Ho! Not until you get rid of those. I am HIGHLY allergic to peanuts.

TAS (to Charlie as she gives the peanuts to John): I'm sorry. I didn't know that.

As Charlie walks off with Tas, John, who is mesmerized with her, suddenly looks at the peanuts in his hand as the lights fade down slightly. John crosses to a table on the other side of downstage. Lights bump up on him at his kitchen counter in his home as he pushes the peanuts into cookie dough on a sheet.

MOTHER (O.S.): Is that oatmeal cookies I smell?

JOHN: I thought I'd bring 'em to rehearsal for everybody.

MOTHER (O.S.): That's so sweet. Why are you putting peanuts in them?

JOHN: Tas likes peanuts.

MOTHER (O.S.): That's so sweet. That girl should be crazy about you. She must be so blind!

John agrees and shakes his head to himself.

Lights out

SCENE 2

Charlie's restaurant; present time. Lights up. SR is a standard commercial kitchen where LENA, 40, is cooking. JOLLY, 50, is making cocktail sauce. To the left is the dining area. An oyster bar at the right, where a velvet picture of Frank Sinatra hangs. US is a private dinning area. Charlie is at the bar cutting out a picture from a magazine. He stops and looks at the walls covered with pictures of him with celebrities. Jolly, walks in through kitchen door with the sauce.

JOLLY: Who's that?

CHARLIE: Charles Bronson.

JOLLY: When he came in here?

CHARLIE: Yesterday. I got a picture of me upstairs that'll blend in with this shot of him. Do ya magic act on it later for me.

Jolly sets the bowl on the bar as he sees Charlie, staring at the wall again.

JOLLY: What are you lookin' at?

CHARLIE: My life, and what it's turned into.

JOLLY: It's mine too. I'm just not in the pictures.

Jolly returns to the kitchen. Charlie smirks then follows him. Jolly dries off trays by sink.

CHARLIE: I know it's yours too, Jolly.

JOLLY: You don't act like it. That's why Tas gets aggravated.

Charlie takes trays from Jolly and stacks them.

CHARLIE: You don't know what it's like, to havin'....

Jolly mimics Charlie, who motions with his fingers to a small size. Jolly's heard it many times before.

CHARLIE (cont'd): ...come this close, to what would have been my life. Then have it stolen away from you!

JOLLY: What are you talking about college again?

Lena watches the both of them and shakes her head to herself.

She goes from stirring the pot on the stove to dumping cans of ketchup into a large bowl.

LENA: What makes you think you woulda had the same success John Goodman had?

Charlie whips around to her and her treacherous thoughts. Jolly is astounded at her boldness.

CHARLIE: Because I was BETTER! I WAS Stanley.

LENA: Oh, you Stanley, alright.

Mutters to herself.

You just ain't no Marlon Brando.

Charlie doesn't hear her but Jolly does and smiles to himself. Charlie sees this and gets aggravated.

CHARLIE: You got something to say, Lena, you say it!

LENA: I'll say it alright, Charlie, don't you think I won't! I'm reading a book right now about people like you. "Obsessive Compulsive People of the Bible."

LENA (cont'd): Moses. Forty years going around some mountain, because he couldn't take them rotten apples into the promised land.

Tas walks down steps that lead into the kitchen.

TAS: Now that's compulsive.

Tas stands at the foot of the steps in the kitchen.

LENA: That's you, Charlie, you're compulsive enough to get all of these pictures. But that don't make you no actor.

Charlie turns red from anger, Jolly gives a flinch.

JOLLY: Lena!

LENA: Charlie, you a oyster man, I'm a cook. The difference is I'm the Marlon Brando of cooks! Instead of just ketchup, lemon and horseradish, I add a little MSG to my cocktail sauce. I make them oysters dance in their mouths. And what about my oyster soup? I add Dixie beer to it.

And you know them customers love my oyster soup.

As Lena turns and stirs her soup, everyone makes faces to themselves.

She spoons out some.

LENA (cont'd): I got to admit, I wasn't a bad actor myself in high school.

CHARLIE: If ya acting is anything like ya soup....

LENA: If you got anything to say to me, Charlie Faucheux, you be a man and say it!

CHARLIE (to himself): I thought I just did.

Lena throws a look at Charlie as BOY sticks his head in the back door.

BOY (to Charlie): James Garner's over at Binder's bakery.

Boy sticks out his hand to Charlie, who whips around to Jolly, who shrugs.

CHARLIE (to Boy): You sure it's him this time?

Jolly crosses to a shelf and takes the camera off of it.

BOY: Yeah.

LENA (to Boy): That's what you said last time about Jackie Gleason.

CHARLIE: You the one who sent me to....

Jolly checks the camera as he crosses to back door.

BOY: No, that was my brother.

LENA: That's a crock. It was you. The man's been dead ten years and you tell him he's havin' brunch at....

BOY: Alright, it was me! But you gotta admit, he looked like Jackie Gleason. I didn't know he was dead. "The Honeymooners", are always on.

CHARLIE: He did look like him.

LENA (to Boy as she motions to Charlie): You must be talking to him. 'Cause you know I ain't buyin' it.

Charlie gives Lena a look, he crosses to Boy, while he pulls out his wallet.

TAS: Charlie, when is enough, enough?

CHARLIE (to Boy): Look, I'll give you two now and three more when I get back, if it's him.

Lights out

SCENE 3

Restaurant, dining area. Lights bump up on a few customers, besides JULIE, 46, cruise line director, and MARTHA, 46, a Los Angeles actors' agent. They sit together at a table and take menus from Jolly, who returns to the oyster bar. He opens oysters with a knife and lays the halves on crushed ice on the round trays.

JULIE: It's the same boring cruise. But I'm not thinking these old people notice it. That's when this elderly lady says, "On the 'Love Boat,' there was always something going on." That's what gave me the idea! You represent all those actors in LA that can't find work. And that's what they did on the 'Love Boat'. They used all THOSE actors.

MARTHA: So it would be dinner theater, just done all over the ship.

JULIE: Exactly.

MARTHA: But you want the tourists, to act with the actors?!

JULIE: Exactly. Maybe improvisation. The tourists would pay for that, let alone being on a cruise. ---We just need some type of hook.

Julie points around at the pictures.

JULIE (cont'd): If we could get actors like these people did....

Lights bump up on kitchen as dinning area action continues. Tas walks behind Charlie, who's doing paper work. Lena cooks as she keeps an eye on them.

LENA: Charlie, they see you comin' a mile away.

CHARLIE: It even sounded like him.

Charlie grabs a try of condiments and walks out to dining area, followed by Tas.

TAS: It always does.

Jolly organizes oyster bar, Charlie puts condiments under the bar. Boy enters from front door, crosses to Charlie, expecting his money. Charlie sees him.

CHARLIE: It wasn't him.

BOY: It sure sounded like him.

Julie and Martha listen in on their conversation.

CHARLIE: I know.

BOY: So, I don't get my money? (Beat) It sure sounded like him.

TAS (to Boy): They all look like HIM.

BOY: Not this much.

Boy exits disappointed.

TAS: Out of all these pictures, you have what, two real ones?

Charlie gives Tas a look.

TAS (cont'd): Charlie, you're the only one who cares about these pictures. Nobody else gives them a second look.

CHARLIE: They look.

TAS: Maybe if ya buddy John hung out here. But when he does come back and has parties, you won't even....

Charlie stops and looks at her.

CHARLIE: You always did like him.

Charlie turns toward the kitchen followed by Tas, who shakes her head to herself.

TAS: It all goes back to "Streetcar." Oh, I just wish you hadn't'a gotten sick.

CHARLIE: If I hadn't'a gotten sick....!

TAS: I gotta go to the French Market.

Lena, working at the stove, looks up to God. Charlie points to a picture of John Goodman on the wall. Jolly points to the same picture, mimicking Charlie. Tas smiles to herself as she sees him.

CHARLIE (cont'd): THAT WOULD BE ME UP THERE! Woman! You wouldn't even know me anymore!

Charlie enters the kitchen, followed by Tas. Lena rolls her eyes as they come in.

LENA (to herself): They had to come back here.

TAS: The worst part is, you don't just humiliate yourself. You have to drag Jolly through the muck with ya!

Charlie's silence as he goes about stacking glasses on a tray makes Lena look at Tas, which makes her feel bad.

TAS: Lena, ya coming with me? What do we need?

Julie motions for Jolly, who crosses to her.

JULIE (to Jolly in a low voice as she motions to the kitchen): Could I be nosey and....?

Tas looks in the over crowded cooler. Lena walks up behind her.

JOLLY: Oh. In college, Charlie was gonna play Stanley in "Streetcar", and when he got sick, John Woodman went on to play it opposite Tas. John went on to be a famous actor. And Charlie....

Jolly motions around, shrugs, then crosses to the kitchen.

JULIE (excited to Martha): Is it me, or did it just write itself?

MARTHA: What are you thinking?

JULIE: We start the cruise from here. We get Charlie to let us setup a Celebrity Cruise Lines booth. Our motto is, "You never know who you are going to sail with."

Julie motions to the pictures, pauses to let Martha take it in. Charlie heads for the bar with the glasses.

JULIE (cont'd): It'll be like a mini Las Vegas--- BRANSON ON THE SEA!! We'll give your clients a chance to work. And we can get 'em dirt cheap at first, to see if it works. That would make my people receptive to it! (Beat) Well?

When Charlie gets at the bar he stacks the glasses on and under it.

MARTHA: I think you'd better check with your cruise line first.

JULIE: They will be gung-ho for anything that brings in the tourists. See if your people will be receptive to it.

TAS: You don't think we're too old to be trying to raise a kid?

Jolly shakes his head no to Lena, who agrees with him. Martha digs out her phone book.

LENA: You might be too old to make one, but you never too old to raise one. Where ya think a kid would rather live? Some place with good people or some place where they beating him with hammers all day long.

Lena notices Jolly looking at her. Tas looks back at Lena.

LENA (cont'd): Ya hear things.

Martha dials a number on her cell phone. Lights rise DS on ABE VIGODA on the phone.

MARTHA: Abe it's Martha. Dinner theater on a cruise line.

Abe's breath is taken away from him.

ABE: So, this is what it's come to. Dinner theater on a---

MARTHA: Abe, crying won't get you work. Besides, it sounds fake.

ABE: You saying I'm a fake? I'm no good as an actor? I'm washed up? I've worked with Neil Simon, Francis Ford....

MARTHA: Abe Vigoda. How would you like to go back to work?

ABE: Am I talking to the wall here?

MARTHA: You have any problem with relocating?

ABE: Poland. I won't play Poland, or Jersey. Not that I got anything against Poland. Jersey, I cannot go back to. I'd rather not talk about it.

MARTHA: Abe.

ABE: I refuse! I DRAW THE LINE AT POLAND! If they woulda stopped Hitler....

MARTHA: I've got to go, Abe. I have to call that sitcom actor, Gary Coleman.

ABE (Beat): Him again?! (Beat) ALRIGHT, I'll go to Jersey!

MARTHA: It's not in Jersey, Abe.

Lights fade down slightly as Abe and everyone else exits. Martha crosses to DS as the lights come up just on her.

MARTHA: GARY, trust me. I know it sounds weird. But, New Orleans is slated for a lot of movies. It's going to be the next Vancouver. I have actors from Star Trek, Gilligan. Who? I got James Doohan, you, Abe Vigoda, Dawn Wells. (Beat) I know you and Abe had problems. I think it's going to work. Let me put the finishing touches on it, and you get your bags packed.

Lights out

SCENE 4

Restaurant. Lights rise on dining are and kitchen. Charlie at the bar, looks at the newspaper. Lena and Jolly look over the Celebrity Cruise Line booth just DS of the bar. Julie is putting finishing touches on the booth.

CHARLIE: Here's our add in the travel section. Celebrity Cruises.

LENA: So people won't know who'll be on the cruise? That's the gimmick?

JULIE: No gimmick.

LENA: Why would you wanna go on a cruise when you don't know who the star's gonna be?

JULIE: We'll use the same people they used on the "Love Boat".

LENA: You liable to end up with the Hulk.

Tas enters from the kitchen. Jolly and Lena take pamphlets from the booth and look at them.

JOLLY: But why start here?

LENA: That little guy that use to say "Da plane, boss, da plane," he's gonna be here?

JULIE (to Jolly as she lies to herself): Because of all the stars that have been in here.

Tas rolls her eyes at Charlie, who shrugs.

TAS (hollers at Lena): LENA, HE'S DEAD!! HOW MANY TIMES I HAVE TO TELL YOU HE'S DEAD, LIKE THE SHOW, DEAD!!

Everyone looks at Tas.

TAS (cont'd): She's got a thing for little guys.

Tas crosses towards Charlie.

LENA: Ya know what they say about big things in little packages.

TAS: Charlie, I wanna talk---

Tas and Charlie move to other end of bar.

CHARLIE: About what?

A tourist couple walk in with a newspaper and gawk at all the pictures. Jolly watches them and shrugs.

TAS: I got some new candles from Pier One.

Tas has Charlie's full attention.

TAS (cont'd) (coquettish): New bubble bath too.

Charlie pretends to grab something behind the bar as he leans by Tas and pretends to bite at her neck.

TAS: I want to talk tonight.

The flags go up to Charlie.

CHARLIE: About what?

TAS: Tonight.

CHARLIE: No. At least give me a hint.

TAS (casually lobs the bomb): What you think about adopting?

CHARLIE (indignant): Kids? Things are finally clicking, and now you wanna.... It's always about you.

Tas glances at Lena, then walks to kitchen. Lena shakes her head at Charlie, then follows Tas. Charlie shrugs, "What?" towards Lena. Lights fade slightly down. As they bump up DS on miscellaneous film equipment, light deflectors. Craft table set up where John Goodman sits with several newspapers, as he looks at one. Several crewman are around.

JOHN (to himself): Charlie? A cruise line? What are you up to now?

John then notices FRED WARD watching him. He's in a trench coat and hat and grimaces like "Humphrey Bogart," as he mimics his voice and gestures. Whenever Fred appears, it will be like this.

FRED: What newspaper's that?

JOHN: It's my home newspaper. The Times Picayune.

FRED: A conscience is a terrible thing. I had mine surgically removed.

JOHN: Aren't you...

FRED: What I was then, ain't necessarily what I am now. Nor should it represent what I will be in the future.

John turns back to crewmen, whose backs are to him. When John turns back to Fred, he's gone. John looks around.

JOHN (to crewmen): Hey.

CREWMAN turns to him.

JOHN (cont'd): Is Fred Ward in this film? The guy who acted in that film with the giant worms.

CREWMAN: Who?

John shakes his head "never mind," then turns back to his newspaper which is gone. The crewmen look at each other and shrug. Across the stage on the other side of the set, Fred Ward looks at John's paper. The lights bump out DS as they come up fully on the dinning area and kitchen where Lena is moving fast. The tables are full of customers that Tas and Charlie wait on. People walk around and look at the pictures on the walls. Jolly shucks oysters at the bar as he gets the customers beer and soft drinks in between. Charlie notices STEVE.

CHARLIE: Anybody ever tell you you look like Steve McQueen?

STEVE: I am Steve McQueen.

CHARLIE: No, really.

STEVE: Really.

CHARLIE: I'm serious, if you're not going to be serious....

Steve gets in Charlie's face.

STEVE: What makes you think I'm not serious. You want to knock this block off?

Steve motions with his shoulder. Charlie looks at Jolly.

CHARLIE: Now ya doin' Robert Conrad.

ABE VIGODA, 70, walks in and looks at the pictures on the wall. He and Charlie look at one another.

CHARLIE: ABE

(simultaneously)

You must be....

They are both taken back with each other. In walks GARY COLEMAN, 30, a very short man. They both look at him then at each other.

ABE (to Charlie): I heard he was coming.

Gary walks towards Abe. They shakes their heads, as they silently acknowledge each other. Lena enters from the kitchen with a tray of food and sets it on the bar. She spots Gary.

LENA (to herself): Lena's ship has come in.

Lena crosses to Gary.

LENA (to Gary): I see they finally got a star in here.

ABE (to Charlie): Have I gone invisible again?

LENA (to Abe): I thought you was dead.

TAS: LENA!

LENA (to Abe): They took you for a ride in that movie.

Lights bump out

SCENE 5

Restaurant. Lights bump up on the cast in the dinning area. Abe, Gary, DAWN WELLS, 55, RUSSELL JOHNSON, 60 and JAMES DOOHAN, 65, are around a table as they eat and sign autographs for customers. Julie shows a WOMAN a pamphlet. Jolly shucks oysters as he watches. Tas waits on tables. Charlie seems aggravated.

GARY (to Charlie): Ohh, Charlie! Would you get us some more of those onion rings.

Julie sees Charlie tries to hide his aggravation. She smiles at him, which makes him soften and exit to the kitchen. Tas sees this and it puts her out. Jolly shakes his head to himself.

ABE (to Julie): Can I get more of that sauce?

Julie crosses to the bar. She steps behind the bar where Jolly motions to the bowls of cocktail sauce.

WOMAN (to cast): So, what play are you rehearsing to put on?

The cast look at one another, then at Julie. Who is picking up a bowl of cocktail sauce as she spots an old copy of the play, "Streetcar Named Desire" on the shelf. Without missing a beat she crosses to the cast with both.

JULIE (to Woman): "Streetcar." I have my copy here. I left the other copies on the ship.

WOMAN: Can I get a picture of you rehearsing?

DAWN: Sure.

Dawn takes the copy from Julie and opens it, she then points out a spot to Gary. Tas notices Jolly staring at them. Tas looks at the cast when she suddenly spots the script in their hands.

GARY (acts and sounds just like Marlon Brando as he reads): I don't care if she hears me!

Tas is crossing to rip the script from their hands, when Charlie enters from the kitchen with the order of onion rings. Tas freezes. Charlie stops at the bar to get napkins.

GARY (cont'd): Now let's see the paper. Did you ever hear of the Napoleonic code, Stella?

Jolly and Tas see Charlie who's back is to Gary. Charlie acts as if a knife was just plunged into his back. He slowly turns and sees Dawn reacting to Gary's reading.

GARY (cont'd): Now, just let me enlighten you to a point or two.

Charlie, who has just been repeatedly stabbed with every word, makes his way with the onion rings to Gary.

GARY (cont'd): Now, what we have here in the state of Louisiana is the Napoleonic Code.

Charlie gets to their table with every intention of taking his script back. With so many wounds, he is only able to set the onion rings down. He then makes his way back to the kitchen.

GARY (cont'd): You see, according to that, what belongs to the wife belongs to....

Charlie exits to the kitchen as lights bump down slightly. Therapist office lights bump up DS, John Goodman is standing as he winds up a session with his THERAPIST, who is walking him to the door.

THERAPIST: Restitution is not for the person you offended. It's for you.

JOHN: I understand. But I have offended so many people.

THERAPIST: You have to start somewhere.

JOHN: I got ya.

John turns to leave then turns back.

JOHN (cont'd): You ever get the feeling you're loved but not necessarily liked.

THERAPIST: You have it backwards. You feel liked, just not loved.

JOHN: No. I get a lot of love. Lots of love. (Beat) But I don't think anybody likes me.

THERAPIST: We're going to have to save this one for next time. Because you are insane. Everybody likes you.

John crosses to the door.

JOHN: Are you supposed to say that to your patients?

THERAPIST: I deal in reality. See ya.

John exits.

JOHN: Okay.

Lights bump out on Therapist as they come up DS on Fred Ward in elevator corridor where John walks up and presses the button for the elevator, Fred is picking his teeth with a drivers license. He still dresses, talks and acts like "Bogart." John walks past him to the elevators. They watch one another.

FRED: If he deals in reality, then you ARE liked and loved.

JOHN: What are you doin', Bogart on me?

FRED: I am Bogart, in a way--- Sister!

JOHN: SISTER!? You sure you should be saying that to someone walking out of a shrink's office?

FRED: I bet you can't say that three times in a row. Look.... What are you doin' in a head-breaker's office, anyway? Nobody feels liked and loved. Ya think Kirk Douglas felt liked and loved in "Detective Story"? He wouldn' a been drivin' himself and Eleanor Parker insane.

JOHN: Are you....

FRED: In the scope of things what does anything matter?

JOHN: Well, put it this way. Am I awake?

FRED: As much as anybody, kid. What I'm gettin' at is, if you owe the piper.... ect., ect....

John tries to make sense of the conversation.

JOHN: Ahh. You must be my conscience?

FRED: Isn't everybody?

Sound of elevator doors opening up.

JOHN: You want a tooth pick?

John gets on the elevator and presses a button.

FRED: No. This is the way my father picked his teeth....

Elevator doors begin to close as the lights fade out.

FRED (cont'd): ....And the way his father....

As the lights bump the rest of the way out DS they come up fully on the kitchen where Charlie puts together an order as Lena cooks.

CHARLIE: These actors are worse than any of the real people.

LENA: So, what does that make them, non-people?

CHARLIE: They're leeches. They're living off the blood of....

Tas walks in and stands behind Charlie, listening.

CHARLIE (cont'd): ....the fame of this place!

TAS: Which is from those people to begin with, Charlie. So, if anybody is living off of anybody, it's you.

Charlie gives Tas a look and walks to the dining room door with the tray and the order on it.

TAS (cont'd): You sure ran out to get those onion rings.

CHARLIE: This isn't about onion rings. I know what this is about.

Charlie crosses back to Tas.

CHARLIE (cont'd) (low voice): What happened to the candles last night?

TAS: If you know what this is about, you know what blew the candles out.

CHARLIE: Oh, I know. I just want you to know, I know and it's inside.

He points at himself.

LENA: If you know what I know, you better take that order inSIDE the dining room before it gets cold.

Charlie exits to dining room as the lights rise in there. Jolly shucks oysters. Gary, on the phone behind the bar. Julie, is working at the booth. At their table, Russell and James eat as Dawn and Abe sit there. Charlie crosses to customer with their order.

TAS: Lena, he's fighting it. That means he thinking about.

LENA: Charlie lives in the, "what coulda been." Me, I'm about my soup!

TAS: What is my thing? (Beat) All I ever wanted was to be married to Charlie and have kids. Maybe that's why I never understood Charlie.

LENA: Mama said, there's those that dream and those that do. Maybe it's time you stop dreamin' and start doin'.

TAS: I thought I was tryin' to do.

LENA: Girl, maybe it's time to get yaself another dream!

TAS: I have a dream!

LENA: Girl, you ain't no Martin Luther King, and look what happened to him!

TAS: On that, I'm goin'.

Gary, sees customers enter the restaurant. Julie catches Gary's look, and sees the customers.

JULIE (to cast): The cocktail sauce is spicy!

The cast look at Julie then the door. Russell and James, both with a mouth full of food, look at Abe and Dawn. Dawn picks up one of several xeroxed copies of "Streetcar." Abe, reluctantly follows her, and turns to the page she is on. The customers spot the cast. Charlie hands out his order as he tries to ignore what the cast are doing.

DAWN (doing "Stella"): Don't you think your superior attitude is a little out of place?

The customers cross to them in awe. Abe looks surprised at Dawn, who suddenly realizes what she has done. Abe accepts his role with a regal air, and follows her lead.

ABE (doing "Blanche"): May I speak plainly. If you'll forgive me?

The customers are thrilled as they watch them rehearse.

ABE (cont'd): He's common. He's like an animal. He has an animal's habits. There's something subhuman about him. Thousands of years have passed him right by and there he is! Stanley Kowalski, survivor of the Stone Age.

The customers applaud as they surround the cast. Charlie crosses to the oyster bar and notices Gary on the phone behind it. Gary sees Charlie is aggravated with him.

GARY (into phone): I got to go.

Julie guides the customers back to the booth. Tas enters, at peace, she smiles at Charlie. He smiles back, quizzically.

GARY (cont'd) (into phone): I'll call you later.

Charlie forgets about Gary, who hangs up and crosses to him.

GARY (to Charlie): I see you're agitated.

Charlie watches Tas go to a customer. She smiles and seems to glide around the customer.

CHARLIE (to Gary): I don't like no one behind the bar.

GARY (Beat): I don't want to be here any more than I'm here, but I'm here. What I'm saying here is.... We're here....

CHARLIE: What does that mean?

Charlie still watches Tas.

GARY: Charlie, Charlie, Charlie.

CHARLIE: What are you doing, Marlon Brando on me? I know Brando.

JOLLY: It sounded Captain Kirkish to me.

CHARLIE (to himself): No. It was Rod Steiger.

GARY: Why do we do the things we do?

CHARLIE: What are you doing, nothing but lines on me?

Charlie watches Tas as she pushes hair back and pins it. She does a double take of him when she notices he watches her. It is almost slow motion.

GARY: Charlie, what do you think an actor does? We're always doing somebody else's lines.

CHARLIE: Is that what ya'll do, sit around that table doing other people's lines?

GARY: Yeah, while we wait for our new lines. We're actors, we're not writers.

Abe crosses to them.

ABE: What's the problem? Is there a problem here? I don't want any problems. I'm too old for problems. I want to know what's in the hot sauce. If I only find out one thing before I die, it's gotta be what's in the hot sauce.

Gary and Charlie look at Abe then resume their conversation.

GARY (to Charlie): Meanwhile, we'll bring in customers for you.

ABE: What? Am I not here? Have I ceased to exist, and no one has told me? (Beat) I HATE when that happens!

Lena sticks her head in from kitchen and looks at Abe.

ABE (cont'd) (to Lena): Thank you.

Russell shakes his head as he motions to the pictures.

RUSSELL (to Dawn): Why them and not us? Just tell me, why them?

CHARLIE (to Gary as he looks at Russell): The customers were here before you. That's why you came here, remember?

ABE: Who came first, the chicken or the egg? It's semantics.

CHARLIE: What's semantics?

ABE: I don't know; I'm not a writer.

Lena shakes her head and goes back in the kitchen.

GARY (to Charlie): I told ya.

ABE: I just wanna know what's in the hot sauce.

RUSSELL: I had all the right schools and training.

JAMES (to Russell): How would you like to stand up against Captain Kirk. Not to mention Nimoi in the background. With....

Mimicking Leonard Nimoi.

"THE Actors Studio"

Slipping into Scottish accent.

I'm tellin' ya man, between both of them, they threw around more names then Hollywood's got LEGENDS!

GARY (as he watches the cast): Look, Charlie. We're used to being pampered a little bit.

DAWN (to Russell and James): You two make me sick. You think any of them compare with HER? Last time I even said her name at a "Gilligan" convention, I got sued.

A man enters and does a double take of the cast as he walks to a table. He then does the same with Abe, who looks behind himself to make sure it's him the man looks at.

RUSSELL: Charlie, can I get more ice tea?

ABE (to Charlie): Is that mint in the ice tea?

Charlie exits to kitchen as Gary smiles at him. Lights bump down slightly. DS, outside of a coffee shop John stirs his coffee as he sees someone off.

JOHN: Again I'm sorry---

A beat; then John waves goodbye.

JOHN (cont'd) (to himself): Restitution.

Fred, consistently as "Bogart," walks up stiring his coffee.

FRED (to John): It's good for the soul. But we never remember the one's we owe the most. It goes back to that contemptuous line about familiarity. (Beat) I've always had nothing but contempt for that line.

JOHN: What are you saying, we never apologize to people we owe the most?

FRED: What do you want, the truth? The truth is a packaged lie! It's like twenty essential minerals and vitamins! The truth is waiting for a ship to come in when you know the docks already been closed!

JOHN: So we know who we owe. We just need to apologize to 'em.

Fred backs away from John as he smiles at him.

JOHN (cont'd): What if we don't remember 'em, and we don't know that we don't remember 'em!

Lights bump out on them and come back up on dining area where CHANTEL, a reporter, holds up the add from the TIMES PICAYUNE, as she and a CAMERAMAN enter. They glance around quickly at the photographs on the walls. Cameraman notices the cast sitting at the table.

CAMERAMAN (low voice to Chantel): There they are.

They both suppress their laughter. The cast, humiliated, pretend not to notice they're being laughed at. Tas waits on a table, she looks from Chantel to the cast. Charlie enters from kitchen and lights up when he sees Chantel.

CHANTEL (to Charlie): Is Julie here?

The cast give each other nervous looks.

ABE: This is trouble. I see it coming.

JAMES: What should we do?

RUSSELL: What can you do?

Cameraman shoots the cruise booth as Charlie walks up to Chantel.

CHARLIE: She just stepped out. She'll be right back.

Cameraman shoots Chantel as Charlie pushes back his hair. Tas smiles to herself about Charlie.

CHANTEL (to camera): This is Chantel, with "The Expose'," and we are coming to you live from-- "Charlie's Oyster" in New Orleans.

Gary gets up then stops. Chantel notices this.

CHANTEL (cont'd): And we're here about the upcoming "Celebrity Cruise." --And we wanted to see your celebrities.

Chantel motions to cast, the Cameraman films them.

CHANTEL (cont'd): We thought they might be.... How should I say....? Alive?

Tas can't believe she said that. Abe rises like he's going to hurt Chantel. Gary holds him back.

ABE: I can take her.

James puts a hand on him.

JAMES (in Scottish voice): There's nothing you can do, man!

The cast look at James as he realizes he let the voice out.

JAMES (cont'd): It slipped out.

CHANTEL: Don't you think this is a joke. Or at least a hoax on the American public.

CHARLIE: American public.

Motions to everyone.

AMERICAN PUBLIC!

Lights rise DS on John as he watches TV in his living room.

CHARLIE: LADY, WE ARE THE AMERICAN PUBLIC!

CHANTEL: So, no one famous has ever actually been in here? I mean.... no one that is.... how do you say....? ...actually employed?

JOHN: Charlie, ya not gonna take that, huh?

The man and woman Tas waits on watch her more then Chantel. Tas, now ready to attack, looks for something to throw. She picks up a Dixie beer bottle. Man and woman give each other the raised eyebrow look. Charlie sees the cast is devastated by this comment. Chantel, then the Cameraman focus on them. Julie enters from outside and is excited to see Chantel and the Cameraman. Abe jumps up to attack Chantel.

ABE: THAT'S IT!

Dawn sees him. Charlie crosses to the oyster bar, while Jolly takes in the scene.

DAWN: GARY, stop him!

GARY: No.

Motions to Abe.

I'm with him.

Dawn looks at Russell and James. They both jump up. Charlie grabs a pint of shucked oysters, as Jolly watches him.

RUSSELL (to Abe): Remember your heart!

Charlie crosses to Chantel. Tas smiles as she sees Charlie.

JAMES (Scottish voice): Aye.

Abe looks at James, who shrugs. Charlie pulls back the collar of Chantel's dress and pours the oysters down it. Julie is horrified. Chantel screams, the Cameraman films her as she runs out the door, past Julie.

CHARLIE (to Chantel): That's "Charlie's Oysters." Remember where you got 'em. (To Cameraman) Did you want some oysters?

The camera moves with the Cameraman, who shakes his head "no" as he exits.

JOHN (to TV): Get 'em Charlie! Don't take it! Tas. Feisty as ever. Ready to protect your man. Maybe he did need you more than me.

John suddenly cocks his head as he remembers something.

FRED (V.O.): But we never remember the ones we owe the most.

DS on oppssite side lights bump up on Jack's bar, Fred watches TV as CHUCK works the bar. The lights slightly dim on other two sets.

FRED (to the TV in "Bogart" voice): Charlie, you've traveled so far for someone who's never left home. If you take it from 'em once, you have to take it from 'em all the time.

Fred raises his glass in a toast to the TV.

FRED (cont'd): I wanna work for you.

To Chuck as he points at the TV.

I'm gonna work for this guy, Chuck.

BARTENDER: Aren't you....?

FRED: What I was, Chuck, am, Chuck, and are, Chuck.... --is nothing to what I will be one day, Chuck.

Bartender shakes his head to himself.

BARTENDER (to himself as he mimics "Bogart"): "Of all the gin joints in the world he's gotta come into Jack's."

Fred does a double-take, one-eyed look at the bartender as the lights fade down on both DS sets and rise hard on the restaurant. Jolly and cast are proud of Charlie, who notices the water he spilled on the floor, he exits to kitchen and comes out and mops the spill, he notices everyone stares at him. He and Tas look at each other.

JULIE: Charlie.

CHARLIE: Maybe next time I'll give her the container.

JULIE: Charlie, that just went out live. National! --live.

Charlie shrugs and exits. Julie's cell phone rings.

ABE (to Julie): That man just showed more dignity and honor than I've seen in a long time.

GARY: Yeah.

JAMES (Scottish voice): AYE. That man's been waiting for his moment for forty years. --And he threw it away for us.

Tas smiles to herself, proud of Charlie. Jolly beams to himself when he sees Tas.

JULIE (to herself): Dignity and honor don't get you free publicity.

James notices the customers look at him in awe. Julie exits outside as she answers the phone. James looks at the rest of the cast.

JAMES: I'm doing the voice again?

The cast all nod affirmatively.

JAMES (in tortured horror): One day I'm going to slip over into Scotty and never come back.

The customers near the cast's table, react by drawing away and turning to the pictures on the wall. Man nudges Woman as Tas finishes taking their order. Abe puts the last of the cocktail sauce on a cracker.

ABE: I gotta know what this stuff is made with.

Tas crosses to the kitchen and exits.

JOLLY: My boy Charlie thinks ya worth enough to give away free oysters so come over here and I'll tell ya.

ABE: Jolly, your boy stood up for us. Here we are using him and....

Abe crosses to the bar as Russell looks at the others.

JOLLY: Let me get some more horseradish.

Jolly exits to the kitchen.

RUSSELL (to himself): That's probably what's kept me from other roles. I think like the Professor.

DAWN: I hate it when you do that. You either have it or you don't. It's called talent.

RUSSELL: You know, you can be quite rude at times. That's probably why you didn't get along with HER.

DAWN: Russell---

RUSSELL: We need a big shot.

Russell gets Abe's attention.

JAMES: How's a big name going to make us look like we're alive?

DAWN: It's not for us, it's for Charlie.

GARY: --So, it doesn't look like he has a bunch of losers hanging out here.

Dawn jumps up from her chair and grabs Gary by the collar.

DAWN: Just because we haven't had a new TV series running doesn't mean we're losers!

Abe growls like a cat as he crosses back to them.

DAWN (cont'd): Suck it in, Abe!

JAMES: Good publicity wouldn't hurt us.

ABE: Jimmy Caan's going to be across the street at La Peniche's tomorrow night. He sneaks in and out over there all the time.

GARY: How do you know that?

ABE: My sister e-mailed me.

DAWN: You have e-mail?

Abe looks at Dawn.

RUSSELL: Why would your sister know?

ABE: He's my godson.

Abe catches them all looking at him.

JAMES: You're, the godfather?

ABE: It's nothing Italian. He's my older sister's boy.

GARY: You have an older sister?

Abe gives Gary a look.

DAWN: Did he get you into film?

ABE: No, I got HIM parts. We're practically the same age.

Abe sees that they don't believe him.

ABE (cont'd): I age a little harder than he does.

GARY: You think you can get him to come over?

ABE: I don't see why not. He owes me.

Jolly enters from kitchen carrying horseradish. He sets it on the bar. Abe crosses to him

JOLLY: This stuff's the key ingredient. It's gotta be prepared horseradish, not sauce. I don't think they make it anywhere else.

Jolly sets lemons, ketchup and hot sauce on the bar then picks up the horseradish.

JOLLY (cont'd): This, ketchup, lemon, and hot sauce.

Lights dim down slightly as they rise on the Therapist office DS. John is standing as he looks out of a window. Therapist sits and watches him.

THERAPIST: I know you didn't come here for the view.

JOHN: When you realize something you have to act on it.

THERAPIST: I suppose you're referring to the restitution.

JOHN: I guess I'm going to have to go back home. Maybe my conscience will stop visiting me.

THERAPIST: You make it sound like a person.

JOHN: Yeah, if you can imagine Fred Ward doin' "Bogart!"

John catches Therapist's look.

JOHN (cont'd): Hey, I can't control how he comes to me!

Lights bump out DS then come back up full on restaurant. Tas and Jolly rush around the busy restaurant. Fred, still in "Bogart" persona, enters and looks around.

FRED: Home.

Tas spots Fred. Julie looks at him from the booth in amazement.

TAS: Great. Just what we need, another actor.

Fred crosses to Tas, like Bogart, in the "Petrified Forest." Tas looks at him very peculiarly.

FRED: Hello.

TAS: Are you...?

FRED: Who knows who we are. --I'm looking for work. Could you use a waiter?

TAS: Very much. But aren't you..?

FRED: Are we ever certain who we are?

TAS: I have no idea. Do you always talk like that?

FRED: Like what?

TAS: Never mind. What brings you in here?

FRED: I've come back to my roots.

Motions around.

I belong here.

TAS (surprised): You're from here?

FRED: Dallas, north side.

TAS (shakes her head agreeing): You belong here.

Julie crosses to Fred.

JULIE: Did Martha send you?

FRED: No, Chuck.

JULIE: Chuck?

FRED: From Jack's.

JULIE: I'm.... You're not in our budget. We can't afford you.

FRED: What budget? How can you put a price on a man?

Fred touches her cheek sensuously. She melts. He suddenly squeezes, stretching her cheek, shaking it as he speaks.

FRED: Sha bubbay. Sha Bubbay.

Julie looks at him as if he were nuts.

FRED: My aunt was a cajun. She used to do that to me every time she visited. I've been waiting my whole life to do that again. The first time I did it, the guy didn't understand.

Julie tries to smile and make an escape.

JULIE: Tas, I closed the booth. I'll see you tomorrow.

Julie backs away from Fred. She picks up her purse by the booth and hurries out the front door. Tas watches her as she moves closer to Fred.

FRED (to Tas): I think she likes me.

TAS: As long as she stays away from Charlie.

FRED: Trust me, kid. Nobody wants Charlie but you. I'm sure ya mother's still trying to figure that one out.

Tas rolls her eyes and walks off, lights dim down as they come up DS on a table in a private dining room of an expensive restaurant, La Peniche, where ANTONIO, the thick accented, immigrant owner, sets a bowl of soup in front of JIMMY CAAN, who takes some medicine.

JIMMY: Thanks.

ANTONIO: You're welcome. It's always a pleasure to see you.

Jimmy tastes the soup and coos.

JIMMY: You, Antonio, are a master. I would tell the world, but then, I wouldn't be able to come here.

ANTONIO: Aah, Mr. Caan, you're my favorite customer. That's why I take care of you. No one ever knows you are here. My help doesn't even know. I made your eggplant perougue myself.

JIMMY: You spoil me, Antonio. You spoil me like a child.

Antonio blushes and walks out to the kitchen. The cast, led by Abe, sneaks in. Jimmy is surprised to see Abe.

JIMMY: Hey, Abe, what's going on?

ABE: Your mother e-mailed me you were going to be over here.

Jimmy looks over the others. He recognizes them one by one. He smiles at them, then turns back to Abe.

JIMMY: What's up?

ABE: I need a favor, Jimmy.

JIMMY: You know if I can, I'd be happy to.

ABE: We're all down here because some work is about to break. I need you to go across the street and be seen eating over there.

JIMMY: Abe, I'm eating here.

ABE: So, you can't eat over there, too?

JIMMY: I came in town especially for this, now you want me to eat, God knows what!

ABE: When I first got you work, and you started working more than me, did I say anything?

JIMMY: Here we go. It all comes back to that.

All of the others feel extremely uncomfortable.

ABE: --And it always WILL, until you pay me that life you owe me!

JIMMY: Wait a minute. That's from a movie. You're doing lines on me?

ABE: Jimmy!

JIMMY: You're doing lines on ME! I invented lines. I might even have said that one. It sounds so familiar.

Abe, raving, paces behind Jimmy.

RUSSELL: Dustin Hoffman.

Jimmy tastes his soup, savoring the flavor as Abe explodes and picks up a chair.

GARY (to Abe): That's a chair.

Jimmy looks at Gary realizing what he's looking at. Abe hits Jimmy, who braces for the blow. The rest of them are horrified as Jimmy slumps onto the table.

ABE (to Jimmy): Look at what you made me do.

DAWN: What are you doing, "Scarface" now!?

Russell searches for a pulse on Jimmy's neck and finds none.

RUSSELL: He's dead.

ABE: He died when I got him that first job years ago.

JAMES (to Abe): Are you insane?

James looks around.

GARY: Actions speak louder than words.

Dawn crosses to the kitchen door and peaks in.

DAWN (turns to them in low voice): Keep it together. (To Russell) Are you sure he's dead?

Russell checks Jimmy's pulse again.

RUSSELL: There's no pulse.

DAWN: Look, no one saw us come in! If no one sees us leave, we were never here!

ABE: I have to e-mail my sister.

Dawn takes the chair from Abe.

JAMES (Scottish voice): But we're talkin' about murder!

They all look at James.

RUSSELL: Can you once get emotional without using that voice?

GARY: I saw it coming.

RUSSELL: When did you see it coming?

GARY: When he picked up that chair.

Dawn leads them out.

DAWN: We all saw it by then, Gary!

Lights bump out. The cast cross back to their table in Charlie's restaurant. The lights come back up on the dining area as they sit around the table and try to be inconspicuous. Fred walks up to their table with menus.

GARY (to Fred): Aren't you....?

FRED (grimaces as "Bogart"): Your waiter! (Beat) Now, what do you want?

Fred hands out menus.

ABE: You?

FRED: Who?

JAMES: Huh?

Jolly enters from kitchen and crosses to bar.

JOLLY (to them): When--

DAWN: What are we doin' "Mamet" here?

FRED: You guys want something to drink, so you won't look like you just "iced" somebody?

DAWN (nervously): Coffee! Coffee for everybody!

FRED: You don't need the caffine sister.

DAWN: I need to be awake.

Imitating Bogart.

Do I look like your sister?

FRED: No, but you sound like my brother.

Fred crosses to bar. Having overheard them, Jolly pulls out coffee cups. Dawn rushes over to bar.

FRED (to Dawn): Did I forget something, my brother?

Dawn looks strangely at Fred as she grabs Jolly's arm.

DAWN (low voice): Jolly, if anyone asks, we never left.

JOLLY: I won't say anything.

Dawn crosses back to table.

FRED (to Jolly): Too much caffeine.

DAWN (low voice to others): I think we're in the clear.

Lights come back up in the kitchen. Lena cooks; Charlie looks out the back door.

CHARLIE: Where's Tas?

LENA: Probably clipping her hair. She's supposed to be washing it. She wants me to color it later.

As the lights dim slightly in the kitchen and dining room, DS streetlights rise on the night with Antonio freting outside the back of his restaurant. Charlie walks up to Antonio, who wrings his hands and freaks out more and more.

CHARLIE (joking): What's the matter, Antonio, you look like someone stole your perougue recipe and they won't give it back.

ANTONIO (desperate): James Cain came to eat here tonight!

CHARLIE (excited): He's in there now?

ANTONIO (crying): Yes, but he's dead!

Lights rise on the opposite side of DS, on Tas and Charlie's apartment above the restaurant. Tas clips her hair in the bathroom, by the window. Something catches her eye across the street, on the ground. When she looks she sees Antonio grab Charlie by the lapels.

CHARLIE: Dead as....

ANTONIO: --DEAD! He's a making no more movies, Charlie.

CHARLIE: Ya sure he's dead?

ANTONIO: I know dead, Charlie! I used to cook for the Mafia! I've seen enough dead people! He's dead! With my past.... They'll never believe.... I'm ruined.

An idea comes to Charlie and he lights up.

CHARLIE: I got an idea. You go back in ya kitchen. Me and Jolly go in through your side door and take him out and bring him to my place. And I'll say he.... ---What did he have, a heart attack?

ANTONIO: I guess.... You.... You'd do this for me?

CHARLIE: If we don't look out for each other, who will?

ANTONIO: You're right. You're right, Charlie. I'll never forget this, never!

Antonio is overflowing with emotion. Tas looks puzzled as she looks out the window. Lights bump out DS. As the lights fade in on Charlie's private dining area US, Charlie and Jolly carry Jimmy's body wrapped in a carpet.

JOLLY: This is very uncool, Charlie.

CHARLIE: It isn't like we killed him.

They set him on the floor. Charlie removes Jimmy from the carpet. They set him on a chair and spruce him up. Jolly stands back amazed, realizes Charlie's plan.

JOLLY: You want him to be found here.

Charlie tries to open Jimmy's eyes but they won't stay open.

CHARLIE: I thought when you died, your eyes remained open.

JOLLY: I thought I heard that too. Why...?

CHARLIE: Where's the Superglue?

Jolly steps back blown away.

JOLLY: Charlie, that's desecration.

Charlie looks queerly at him then walks to the door that leads to the dining area.

CHARLIE: That's what you do a grave.

Charlie walks into the main dining area as the lights go up in there. The cast jumps, startled when they see Charlie, which makes him jump.

ABE: What?

CHARLIE: What?

GARY: What?

CHARLIE: You guys okay?

CAST (simultaneously): Yeah!

Charlie looks suspiciously at them, then at Fred who's watching the bar. Fred raises his eyebrows.

CHARLIE (to Fred): Is it me?

FRED: It's always you, Charlie, it's your oyster. But it's the new moon that has everyone.... New moon, new beginnings.

Charlie acknowledges this then exits to kitchen area where the lights bump up. Lena drags garbage out the back door. Charlie searches around kitchen as Tas stands in doorway that leads to upstairs.

LENA (to them): Hey, what good is the new guy if he don't help with things like this?

As Charlie glances at Lena, he sees Tas. Lena shakes her head as she sees they don't even hear her.

CHARLIE (to Tas): Is it me, or is that new waiter freaky?

LENA: I guess I'm talking to myself.

Lena carries out garbage.

LENA (cont'd) (to herself): Freaky like a fox. He ain't carryin' the garbage out.

TAS: What you lookin' for, Charlie?

Charlie stops and looks at her.

CHARLIE: Nothing.

TAS: Charlie, what's going on?

CHARLIE: Nothing.

TAS: Charlie, we have to talk sometime.

CHARLIE: Tas, now is not the time.

Charlie finds Superglue then sees a black marker that he puts in his pocket. Fred stands with the door to the dining area cracked open. He listens.

TAS: I have stuck with you, through no customers. Now you're going through this Frank Sinatra "Rat Pack" thing. --And I got Bogart waitin' on tables! Where's it gonna end, Charlie? I know what this is all about. ---OH, I WISH you would'a played Stanley, so you could'a seen there was nothin' to it!! --John Woodman just lucked out!

CHARLIE: WHAT MAKES YOU THINK I WOULDN'T OF LUCKED OUT!? IT WAS MY TURN!

Charlie turns to leave. Fred pulls back slightly, leaving the door closed almost completely.

TAS: Why can't you just be happy with what you have?

Charlie stops and looks at her.

CHARLIE: I am.

TAS: Stop trying to capture some sort of fame that was never meant to be.

Charlie walks to dining room door.

TAS (cont'd) (Beat): What did you carry into the back room?

CHARLIE: Nothing.

TAS: You've got a lot of nothing's, Charlie, ya know that?

CHARLIE: Sometimes nothin's all ya got.

TAS: Like us?

CHARLIE: I didn't say that, Tas.

Charlie turns back to Tas.

CHARLIE: We always had something. Was I wrong for wanting more?

TAS: Was I?

CHARLIE: Maybe if you'd a chosen John instead of me, you'd a had more. Is that it, Tas?

TAS: What are you talking about?

CHARLIE: What, you think I'm stupid? I knew you and John had something going between you.

TAS: Who am I with, Charlie? I could've been with somebody like him.

CHARLIE: Instead of a loser, like me?

TAS: I never thought of you as a loser. Only you think of you as a loser.

Fred pulls away from the door. Charlie shakes his head in defeat then turns and walks into dining area. Tas slumps and sighs as she walks upstairs. The whole cast watches Fred walk back behind bar, they try to not seem suspicious as they pretend to be preoccupied with different things and not notice Charlie walk through to the private dining area. Fred watches this. Charlie crosses to Jimmy who sits motionless at a table as Jolly paces. Fred crosses to the private dining area. He quietly cracks the door open and looks in. Abe walks up to him as the rest of the cast watch.

ABE (low voice): Why are you spying on them?

FRED (low voice): When I was in the service I wanted to extend my leave. So I had a friend push an I-beam over on my foot. That didn't work, so I had another friend smash it with a piece of plate metal. I'm lucky to have had friends like that. If you don't go sit down, I'm gonna be a friend to you.

ABE: I got war stories.

Abe turns to walk away.

ABE (cont'd): I just don't wanna talk about them.

Abe crosses back to the cast and is seated.

DAWN (to Abe): What did he say?

ABE: He doesn't need any friends.

Charlie repeatedly tries to open Jimmy's eyes.

JOLLY (pleads): I can't stand being locked up. I hate small places.

CHARLIE: You're not going to be arrested. Go get ya camera.

JOLLY: You said that the last time I was arrested. That was just stalking, this is....

CHARLIE: Who gave you....?

JOLLY: --a job when no one else would? Charlie, how long do you think that one's good for?

CHARLIE: I was hoping to get a few more years out of it.

JOLLY: This is it, Charlie. Carrying around dead people is it. No more.

As Jolly crosses to the door, he notices Charlie uses the marker to paint eyes over Jimmy's eye lids.

JOLLY: You're painting eyes on him?

CHARLIE: I can't get 'em to stay open.

JOLLY: Where's it gonna end?

CHARLIE: What are you talking about now?

JOLLY: Where does it end? Where does reality end and --this world take over. Don't you have any respect?

CHARLIE: Did you see the first few movies he made! Don't talk about respect. He didn't have any, he couldn't of!

Gary crosses casually to Abe and grabs him by the lapels. Fred's attention is divided between them and the other room.

GARY: Why!? Why!? We were so close to getting our lives back!

JAMES: What life?

ABE: He made me do it.

RUSSELL (to James): The life Gilligan stole from me!

DAWN: ENOUGH! ALL OF YA!

FRED (to himself as he looks at Dawn): Feisty.

ABE: Ever since he was a kid with that look.

Abe imitates Jimmy. Fred steps away from the door, and Jolly enters from other dining area. The cast tries to act indifferently, which makes them appear even stranger to Jolly as he exits to kitchen. Fred resumes peeking in the other room, as he watches the cast.

RUSSELL (panic stricken): He knows! I know he knows!

The others try to calm Russell who hyperventilates.

JAMES (Scottish voice): Calm down, man!

The others look at James, who shrugs. Charlie steps back and looks at Jimmy. Jimmy's eye lids are closed and his eyes have been drawn in with a marker. Charlie shakes his head "no" to himself as he looks at Jimmy. He then pulls super glue out of his pocket. As he opens it, it drips on Jimmy's eyebrows.

CHARLIE (to himself): Awe man.

Charlie's fingers become stuck to Jimmy's eyebrow as he tries to wipe it off. Fred chuckles as he steps away from the door. Lena enters kitchen from outside. Jolly sees her as he enters dining room with the camera and notices the cast around Russell. They all jump startled, and again try to appear indifferent as Jolly exits to the private dining area. Fred peeks in again. Jolly looks amazed at Charlie whose fingers are stuck to Jimmy's eyebrow.

CHARLIE: I'm stuck. What removes super glue?

JOLLY: What?

CHARLIE: I was trying to super glue his eyes back!

JOLLY: To keep 'em open? Charlie, how desperate are you?!

CHARLIE: Let me see, my fingers are super glued to the eyebrow of James Cain, who's dead.

JOLLY: We have paint thinner in the back, let me go get it.

Fred steps away from the door. Jolly enters as the cast watch him. He shrugs and exits to kitchen. A CUSTOMER and his WIFE see Abe and walk up to him.

CUSTOMER: Aren't you....?

ABE: Not now.

CUSTOMER: But you are....?

ABE: You know what you are? You're dead. One more word, and you'll be my next victim.

DAWN (to Customer): I'm sorry....

CUSTOMER: You're...?

DAWN: Yes, I am, but this is a private party and....

CUSTOMER: Ohh. Okay, I'm sorry.

CUSTOMER'S WIFE: She's sweet. Just like she was on "Gidget." He's just as nasty as he was on the show.

Customer and wife exit.

ABE: I wasn't nasty on--

Catches himself.

It was a television show!

FRED (to Abe): So, you wacked him?

ABE: What do you know?

The cast is all ears.

FRED: I know trouble, and I know danger. I know you don't get one without the other. --And if you do, you got trouble trying to figure out where it stops and starts.

DAWN (to Abe): What?

ABE: We got trouble.

JAMES (to them as he looks at Fred): And danger.

Fred nods in agreement with James. Gary snaps and goes after Abe, the others pull him off. Lena cleans vegetables as she listens to Jolly in a storage area offstage root around.

JOLLY (O.S.): THERE! I knew you were in there!

Jolly enters with a can of paint thinner. Lena looks at him.

LENA: What are....?

Jolly continues to the dining room door.

JOLLY: Lena don't ask. Don't anything.

LENA: I gotta ask one thing. Is the new guy weird or is it me?

Fred enters private dining area and crosses to Charlie.

FRED: It ain't gonna work, Charlie. Somebody's always tryin'....

CHARLIE (slightly nervous): ---Hey! I didn't kill him.

FRED: I know you didn't, Charlie. Guys like you don't have it in ya. I meant the marker. It never looks real.

CHARLIE: Ya not surprised about....?

FRED: About you being glued to James Cain's eyebrow? Or the fact it's James....?

Charlie motions to the latter.

FRED: Guys like him have been asking for it their whole lives. Now when Barbra Striesand got it from Elizabeth Taylor.... --That surprised me.

Charlie just looks at him.

CHARLIE: I found him across the street.

FRED: That's usually how it happens.

Cast watches Jolly walk through to the private dining area with the paint thinner. After Jolly exits, Lena enters and crosses to the private dining area. Jolly jumps startled when he sees Fred with Charlie.

FRED: Don't mind me, Jolly.

Jolly pours paint thinner on a dinner napkin.

FRED: Charlie, ya don't need paint thinner. Just pull ya finger off, he ain't gonna feel it.

Charlie shrugs, then pulls at his fingers attempting to pull them away from Jimmy's eyebrow. Lena enters and watches them. Charlie jumps.

CHARLIE: I think he flinched.

FRED: Deadmen don't flinch.

Lena realizes Jimmy's dead, she freaks out and runs out, Jolly drops the napkin and runs after her. Fred stops him. The cast watch a terrified Lena run to the kitchen.

FRED (to Jolly): I'll talk to her.

The cast watches Fred walk stiffly like Bogart in "The Petrified Forest." He grimaces to them as he tries to make light of it as he goes after her. After he exits to kitchen, the cast all walk into private dining area. The cast look at each other unbelieving. Charlie attempts to make light of it, as Jolly puts the napkin on Charlie's fingers that are stuck to Jimmy's eyebrow.

CHARLIE: I know this looks a little weird. First of all I didn't kill him.

Fred has Lena cornered.

LENA: That's James Cain in there!

FRED: I know it looks strange. It always does.

Lena picks up a pot in self-defense.

FRED (cont'd): But before you hit me with that pot.... I remember the first time I saw a man glued to another man's eyebrow.

Thinking to himself.

Or was it his ass?

LENA: He wouldn't pose for Charlie so he killed him?

FRED: Nah, ya way off. He was already dead. He died a long time ago. Charlie found him across the street.

Fred looks at knives that are out on the table. Lena sees this, and tries not to let on she is scared, especially when he emphasizes certain words with the knife he picked up.

FRED (cont'd): Don't tell anyone, alright? I might have to use this.

Charlie tries to pry his fingers from Jimmy's eyebrow

CHARLIE: So, that's why I was trying to make him look like he was still alive because he died before I even gave him the entree.

RUSSELL: Where's the soup and salad?

CHARLIE: What, ya think I'm giving you a story?

Charlie's fingers pull away Jimmy's eyebrow taking it with his fingers. They all make faces at this. Jolly hands Charlie the napkin.

GARY: Charlie, nothing personal, but why would this man come to New Orleans... --and come to eat here?

Charlie tries to wipe the eyebrow hair and the super glue off of his fingers.

CHARLIE: What are you trying to say, I brought a dead man in here to get publicity? The man had a heart attack right there! I was just getting pictures of him being in my restaurant.

DAWN: Charlie, look at his head.

Dawn looks at Abe.

ABE: He died across the street where you got him at. He's my nephew, I hit him in the head.

CHARLIE: He's you're nephew!?

Lena makes her way slowly to the steps.

LENA: I got to go help Tas color her hair.

FRED: Above all don't let her find out.

LENA: I got ya.

Fred crosses back to private dining are and enters with the knife, and sees Charlie is free.

FRED: I guess you don't need this.

The cast looks at Fred, then at Jimmy, then back at Fred.

CHARLIE (to Abe): You hit him in the head?

ABE: I asked him to do me a favor.

CHARLIE: So, you killed him!?

GARY (to Charlie): He did it for you.

JAMES (to Charlie): He was trying to get him to come over here and eat.

CHARLIE (to Abe): When he wouldn't come over here to eat.... You killed him?

ABE: We haven't been close since his career took off.

DAWN (to Charlie): Look, you have to bring him back across the street.

RUSSELL: There is no other way, Charlie.

Lights dim down then rise DS on Tas's bathroom with her hair being colored by Lena, who tries to act normal as she watches out the window. The lights rise DS on the other side of the stage where Charlie, Jolly and Fred carry the body wrapped in carpet to Antonio's back door. Charlie notices the back door is cracked open and Antonio peaks out.

CHARLIE: Antonio?

ANTONIO: Charlie, what are you doing?

CHARLIE: I've been thinking, Antonio. I was thinking of myself. There would be great publicity for James Cain to die eating in your restaurant.

And I was trying to get it for myself and that ain't right. So, here. You take him back.

ANTONIO: That's okay, Charlie, I don't want the publicity you keep him.

Antonio closes the door.

FRED: Let me talk to him.

Fred drops his part of Jimmy's body, leaving Charlie and Jolly struggling as they look at one another. Fred crosses to the door.

FRED (through door): Antonio. (To himself) I love that name. (Back to Antonio) Antonio. You don't understand the way things are.

ANTONIO (O.S.): Who are you?

FRED: Nobody. Just a flea on the back-side of the world. I just wanna say, later.... things won't always seem as important as things did when you in the middle of things.

ANTONIO (O.S.) (pause): I got to go now, Charlie.

Lena stops coloring Tas's hair as she watches Charlie, Jolly and Fred. This gets Tas's attention, who watches them with Lena. Charlie, Jolly and Fred are frozen.

ANTONIO (O.S.): Are you still there, Charlie?

CHARLIE (Beat): Yeah.

ANTONIO (O.S.): You must go now, Charlie. I.... I have to go back to work. I can't handle this.

CHARLIE: The truth is, Jolly's done time, and he can't be around a body. They'll think he's at it again.

Fred looks at Jolly, who looks at Charlie. Charlie shrugs to Jolly.

ANTONIO (O.S.): Jolly's a.... I'm sorry. I'm sorry, Jolly, but I can do nothing.

CHARLIE (Beat): The real truth is he was killed in your place.

ANTONIO (O.S.): I know. I told you he was.

CHARLIE: No, Antonio. Someone hit him in the head. He's bleeding from the head.

ANTONIO (opening the back door): He wasn't bleeding when he left this place! ---No, no, no, no! If he was bleeding, he must have come to in your place, and you murdered him. --To --To get pictures, you murdered him?! What kind of man are you?!

CHARLIE: You told me he was already dead!

ANTONIO: What I know, I'm a cook?

FRED: --I know for a fact he was murdered in your place, because Abe Goda is his uncle and he did it.

ANTONIO: I know that name.

CHARLIE: He was in that TV show "Hill Street Blues."

JOLLY: "Barney Miller."

ANTONIO: Fish! Fish, is James Cain's Uncle?

FRED: Well, Abe Goda is. Look, Antonio, we got a dead James Cain here. We can't just....

ANTONIO: Fish kill him, let Fish bury him.

Antonio closes the door; watches Fred. Charlie and Jolly look at one another.

ANTONIO (O.S.): Have you left yet?

Charlie shakes his head.

CHARLIE: Where am I supposed to go, Antonio?

ANTONIO (O.S.): I make a deal with you. You take him back to your place, and I'll have my friends come and get rid of the body.

FRED (to Charlie): Sounds like the best deal ya gonna find under the circumstances.

Charlie and Jolly shrug. Fred helps them walk back to Charlie's place with Jimmy's body as the lights in the street bump out.

TAS: What's going on? Did the old guy, Abe Goda, die?

LENA: No.

TAS: Okay. Is that a body? Did someone die? (Beat)

(To herself) Of course it is. Who sneaks back and forth with a rug. Oh, Charlie, what now?

As the lights bump out on Tas's bathroom they rise up on the private dining area. The cast watch as Jolly, Charlie and Fred walk towards a table with the body in the rug.

ABE: Maybe I can write my memoirs while we're in jail.

GARY: We?

JAMES: Why is it we?

DAWN: Yeah, you freak out and hit him and it's "we did it!"

ABE: Excuse me, I thought we had some kind of camaraderie going on here.

DAWN: Right. To the death house.

ABE: So, you want me to turn myself in?

GARY: No. But if anyone is an accessory, it's them.

Gary motions to Charlie, Jolly and Fred who lay the rug with Jimmy down. Unknown to them Tas enters from dining area followed by Lena.

CHARLIE: Accessory? Did someone say accessory?

GARY: All I said....

CHARLIE: What about the murderer?

ABE: He made me furious.

FRED: Calm down, girls.

JAMES (to Charlie): He wouldn't be here if you hadn't'a carried him over here, seeking publicity!

RUSSELL (to Charlie): Are you that desperate for attention?

JOLLY: What about all of you? Why are ya'll down here?

DAWN: Everything would be fine if he--

Everyone motions to Abe.

DAWN (cont'd): --hadn't'a freaked out.

FRED: Everyone loves pointing fingers. There comes a time in a man's life when he has to stand tall and point the finger at himself. And hopefully it won't be THE finger.

Tas walks towards Jimmy. The others are quiet as they become aware of her.

TAS: Who?

Tas peaks under the rug.

TAS (cont'd): You killed JAMES CAIN?!

They all point at Abe.

FRED: There ya go, pointing the finger again.

ABE: He goaded me.

TAS (to Charlie): And you brought him in here for publicity.... --twice?!

CHARLIE: It started out....

TAS: I don't want to hear it. I'll call the police. If it was an accident. It was an accident.

Tas turns to leave as everyone looks at one another in a panic. Abe looks to the side in the direction of a chair.

GARY (to Abe): Don't even look at that chair.

Everyone looks at Abe. Tas and Lena look back at Abe as they walk out of the door.

DAWN (to Abe): What do you think, this is "Murder She Wrote?"

ABE: I was not looking at a chair. I was reflecting on what has happened. What am I, a sudden mass murderer?

Charlie crosses to the back door and peaks out over at "La Peniche."

FRED (to Charlie): Forget about it. Antonio ain't sending nobody. The only help you got is here and now. Two things we can do. One, put him in a meat grinder.

Fred catches everyone looking at him.

FRED (cont'd): Hey, he ain't in no misery.

Dawn rolls her eyes at Fred.

FRED (cont'd): You got something else, ponytail?

CHARLIE: I know Tas has called the police by now.

DAWN: Let's stick him in somebody's car, and leave him there until the police leave.

Everyone shrugs as the lights fade down. The grumbling cast carry the body

DSR. As the dim street light comes up Jolly, Charlie and Fred situate Jimmy in the front seat of a car. The sound of a police siren can be heard as it nears. Jimmy keeps falling over.

DAWN (to Gary): You crouch down in the back and hold him up, so he looks alive!

FRED: Ponytail's just taking over.

GARY: Whose car is this?

DAWN: I don't know, that's why we're not putting him in the trunk.

JAMES: What happens if the owner comes back?

DAWN: That's why you could never be Kirk!

JOLLY: He was an engineer.

DAWN (whispers to Jolly): Did I press your talk button?! DID I.... --- press your talk button!!?

Everyone draws back. Gary crawls in the back seat of the car and grabs Jimmy by the shirt and holds him back against the seat. Jolly and Charlie push the rug on the side of the car.

FRED: Hold it, Sally, before you turn Betty Davis on me.

GARY: What if someone does come up?

DAWN: Have you heard of improvisation?!

Fred heads them to the back door.

FRED (to Gary): I'll keep an eye on ya. If anyone comes up he's sleeping one off.

Gary nods in agreement. They cross back to private dining area. Police lights are seen as the street light grows dimmer.

GARY (to himself): I didn't kill him, ya Honor. I'm just a black man from a old dead television series... With a successful white, DEAD MOVIE STAR!

As the cast start to murmur Dawn squelch's it. The lights bump up in both dining areas and kitchen, the cast seem to play musical chairs as they try to sit. Jolly, Charlie and Fred look out the door to the regular dining area where Lena and Tas stand by the bar. When the cop lights are seen flashing, Fred exits to the main dining area, as Charlie and Jolly close into the private dining area.

TAS: I think the cops are here.

FRED: You don't know nothin', unless you want ya ol' man to go to the five and ten, and it won't be Woolworth.

TAS: I don't like you.

FRED: I don't like me either, but I'm all I got. I like the way ya old man surrounded himself with tough broads. Ya better watch it though. You could take away his manhood. I knew a guy it happened to. It wasn't pretty.

Lena shakes that one off and walks into the kitchen. Police officers TERRAL and LENNOX enter and look around. Tas walks up to them.

TERRAL: Looks kinda quiet for a homicide.

Tas sees Fred cock his head as he shakes it to himself, doing a, "I told ya so number".

TAS: Excuse me.

TERRAL: Someone reported a homicide.

TAS: Here?

TERRAL: Yes, a Mr. James Cain.

Lennox looks around.

TAS: The actor?

TERRAL: I don't know of any others, do you? You don't mind if we look around?

Lena takes a spoonful of her soup. She makes faces, unable to decide if it's good or bad.

LENA (to herself): I don't know. (Beat) The cops. They eat everywhere.

Lena spoons out some into cups. Meanwhile, Lennox opens the door and enters private dining area, he recognizes all of them. Terral sees Lennox and follows him in and suddenly realizes who they are.

TERRAL (to cast): Mr. James Cain was here?

FRED: James who?

DAWN: What?

ABE: Never heard of him.

The cast all look at Abe, then Terral and Lennox.

JOLLY (to police): They don't have any lines. They need' em, or they don't know nothing.

RUSSELL (to police): Not a thing.

JAMES (to police in Scotty's voice): Absolutely nothing, man!

They all look at James.

LENNOX (to James): You really are Scottish?

JAMES: No. I'm from the Bronx.

TERRAL: So, why are ya'll here and Mr. James Cain's not?

DAWN: We're part of Celebrity Cruise Lines. It's experimental. A live theater, "Love Boat" thing.

TERRAL: So, you're saying he wasn't in here tonight.

RUSSELL: No. Why would he be?

Lennox gets Terral on the side.

LENNOX: I believe the Professor.

TERRAL: That was TV.

LENNOX: I still kinda believe him.

TERRAL (to Jolly and Charlie): What's up with you two?

CHARLIE: We work here.

LENNOX (to Fred): Where do I know you from?

FRED: You ever been in the Pacific?

TERRAL: What does that mean?

FRED: I don't know.

CHARLIE: He's been working here too.

Terral and Lennox look at Fred suspiciously as they cross to the regular dining area. As the lights dim slightly in the restaurant and kitchen the street lights grow brighter on Gary still hiding in the car behind Jimmy holding him back. A car door is heard closing.

GARY (low voice to himself): What are you in for? You're never gonna believe it.

Julie, haven gotten out of her car walks by their car and pretends not to notice Jimmy. She stops and excitedly turns back to Jimmy.

JULIE: I'm sorry, but aren't you, Mr. James Cain! (Beat) You weren't coming into Charlie's Oyster, were you?

Undaunted by no response from Jimmy.

JULIE (cont'd): I don't mean to be an annoyance, but we are trying to--

Gary's grip on Jimmy's shirt loosens and Jimmy falls forward. Gary quickly pulls his hand back. Julie finally notices that Jimmy fell forward and is dead. Julie screams as the lights bump out on the street and come up full only on the dining area. Terral and Lennox are at the front door with a cup of soup each, Lena forces it on them.

TERRAL: We really did just eat.

LENA: Just a taste. You guys eat everything. (Beat) You know what I mean.

They both taste it and want to spit it out, but swallow it instead, as they hand her back the bowls.

LENA: Didn't work, huh?

Lights come up full on private dining area with Gary, panic stricken.

GARY: JULIE SAW JAMES CAIN'S DEAD!! SHE RAN TO THE FRONT TO TELL THE COPS!!

Fred motions to Jolly and Charlie.

FRED (turns back to cast): Remain calm. (To Charlie) While they going out the front lets bring Jimmie into the kitchen, we'll put him on ice.

Fred leads Gary, Charlie and Jolly out the side door as they look at him peculiar.

FRED: In the cooler.

Dawn closes it as the rest of them sit around the table and wait. Terral and Lennox look at Lena as if she tried to poison them.

LENNOX: What was that?

TERRAL (to Lena): No, not at all.

LENA: Big Shot, creme soda. Great drink, just don't work in oyster soup.

LENNOX: Do you try these things before you give them to other people?

LENA: I can't taste anymore, my taste buds are shot.

Julie flies in and is suprised to see the police, but runs up to Terral and Lennox.

JULIE: James Cain's dead!

TERRAL: You the one that called up?!

JULIE: What?

LENNOX: Where?

JULIE: Outside.

Julie hurries outside followed by Terral and Lennox. Lights bump up on Charlie as he rearranges the overcrowded cooler, Jolly, Fred and Gary hold Jimmy. Charlie gets a small spot in the corner clear. They try to get Jimmy to stay there but he keeps falling over.

JOLLY: He's not gonna stay there.

A meat hook is above Jimmy's head, and a near empty sack of onions are on the floor. Charlie picks up the sack of onions.

CHARLIE: I got it.

FRED: What ya gonna do with the onions, Charlie?

Charlie dumps the onions in a pan that has strawberries in it.

FRED (cont'd): Those onions are never gonna come out'a those strawberries.

They all look at Fred as Charlie ties the sack around Jimmy's wrists. Gary and Jolly look at one another about Charlie.

CHARLIE: Help me.

As Charlie picks up on Jimmy's arms, they all notice the hook above. They all then help hang Jimmy from the meat hook. They exit the cooler.

JAMES: I'm too old to go to jail.

RUSSELL: If you were younger, would it make a difference?

ABE: Probably.

DAWN: I'M NOT TAKING THE RAP FOR YOU, OLD MAN!!

ABE: Before it goes any further, I'm going to turn myself in.

Fred, Jolly, Gary and Charlie walk out of the cooler.

CHARLIE: I think we got away with it.

FRED: You got away with it. You got away with more then you know.

CHARLIE: What are you talking about?

They stop in the kitchen.

FRED: You. It's always been about you. There's no room inside of you but for you. --And you's all you got to live with.

Jolly and Gary are freaked out by this and leave the kitchen. Gary looks at Lena and Tas and crosses to private dining area. They want to ask what is going on but don't. Jolly sees them look at him.

JOLLY (to them): I can't talk about it.

CHARLIE: I never know what you're talking about.

FRED: Yeah, me neither half the time. But this time ain't one' a those times. You've been chasin' that stupid dream called Hollywood. It should be called Moneywould, but it ain't because money can't, it never could.

CHARLIE: What are you talking about? Before I die, I would like one time to....

FRED: What are you doin', the Old Man now? Ya pulling an Abe Goda on me? --I'm saying those pictures ain't real. Ya wife is. She always has been.

CHARLIE: I know.

FRED: You gotta let life go. What will be, will be. It's one great big Doris Day song. It's not about puppies and love. It's about a man, a woman and a restaurant. It coulda been a kid if you had of been makin' love to her instead of the restaurant.

CHARLIE: Alright, I get it. I get it. Don't go any further. You've gone far enough.

FRED: I know, that's my problem. Now, I gotta go pick somebody up at the airport. I'll be back in a little bit.

Charlie looks oddly at Fred, who walks to the dining room door. Lena walks in from the dining area.

LENA: Charlie. You know in the past all my men were murderers. I'm even one, if ya count my first husband.

FRED: So, what ya getting at sister, ya danced with death before?

CHARLIE: What, Lena? I'm kinda in the middle of something.

Fred, Charlie then Lena walk into dining area.

LENA: Was that eyes drawn on James Cain?

FRED: It wasn't lips, Lena.

CHARLIE: Lena, it was to make him look like he was awake.

LENA: That's desecrating a....

JOLLY: That's what I said, Lena.

CHARLIE: It was a stupid plan.

Lena turns back to the kitchen.

LENA: Ya can't be mocking death--

Lena enters the kitchen.

CHARLIE: Just don't go in the cooler.

Lena looks at the cooler, than back over her shoulder at them. As she goes about her work she keeps an eye on the cooler. Lights fade in DS around the car as Terral and Lennox look around as they watch Julie circle the car, not finding Jimmy. Charlie sees Tas looking at him, stops to say something to her.

CHARLIE (to Tas): I'll be back.

Charlie exits to the private dining area as Fred, puts on his trench coat.

FRED (shrugs to Tas): It's a start.

Jolly shrugs agreeing with Fred, who crosses to Tas.

FRED (cont'd): You okay, kid?

TAS: I suppose it had to come to this.

FRED: What, murder?

TAS: My husband running after fame, until he catches a famous person and kills him.

FRED: He didn't kill 'im. The old man did. In a family that screwed up it was bound to happen sooner or later. It'll be alright. Trust me. You just have to be there, kid, when it kicks in that you're all he really needs.

Tas looks at him and smiles. Fred's attempt to tap her on the jaw turns into a shove that knocks her to the ground.

FRED: Sorry, kid. I gotta pick up somebody at the airport.

TERRAL (to Julie): Did you call 911?

JULIE: I didn't have time. I just ran inside.

LENNOX: No, he means earlier?

JULIE: I just found him.

TERRAL: You sure this man was dead?

LENNOX: Let's go inside and we'll get a statement from everyone.

The cast sits around the table despondent. Lights bump out DS only.

ABE: Charlie, I'm going to turn myself in.

CHARLIE: Nobody do anything yet. That's ridiculous. You're too old to go to jail. You'd die in there.

ABE: That's the kindest thing anyone's said to me in years.

Lights dim in restaurant and come up DS with sounds of an airport corridor. Fred waits as several passengers walk by with their luggage. John walks up with his bag surprised to see Fred.

FRED (to John): Everyone got off the boat. I thought you missed your flight.

JOHN: You following me?

FRED: The hard way. In front ya. Walk this way.

As Fred walks away like Bogart in the "Petrified Forest." He notices John isn't following him. John notices people watching.

JOHN: I can't walk that way. I'm too big.

Fred motions "along this way." John shakes his head understanding. Fred glances up to God, which John catches.

JOHN: You looking up to HIM (motions to God) over ME!?

FRED: Hey, you the guy who thinks he's talking to Bogart!

People look at both of them.

JOHN: You're imitating him!

FRED: What you know you could put in a pack of ketchup.

JOHN: I don't have to take this from you.

FRED: You'll take it and you'll like it! And you know why? Because you think you're talking to yaself. --And that's why these people are looking at ya. They're lookin' at ya because you are you and I'm me, and we don't know who they are!

JOHN: What are you talking about? Does anyone ever know what you are talking about?

FRED: I think Doris Day did once, but I wasn't ever really sure.

Lights bump out DS as they come up full on the whole restaurant. In the private dining area Terral and Lennox take statements from the cast as Charlie, Tas, Jolly, Lena and Julie look on.

TERRAL (to Abe): Did you call 911?

ABE: I don't use phones. I don't use horns either. I roll down the window and holler.

They all look at Abe. Terral turns to Gary.

TERRAL: How about you?

ABE: I don't like the noise.

Terral, who turned back to Abe, now turns to Gary.

ABE (cont'd): I think it's because I have a ringing in my ears.

Terral, who refused to look over at Abe, now looks at him to see if he's done. Abe senses this, and motions, go ahead. Abe rolls his eyes at this. Terral sees this, and though agitated turns back to Gary.

TERRAL: Did you call 911?

GARY: No. The last time I did, it was by mistake, I was trying to get information. They came out and recognized me. They thought I was wanted so they dragged me off.

JAMES: I hear ya there. If had a nickel for every time they dragged me out in my draws....

They all look at James as he realized what he said.

TERRAL (turns to Dawn): Did you call 911?

DAWN: I don't know the number.

Julie, frustrated, walks out in a huff to the dining room. She looks behind the bar and grabs a two liter cola and pours it into a glass and tastes it. Lena, bored, exits and see Julie.

JULIE (to herself): Flat.

Julie walks into the kitchen and enters the walk-in cooler and looks around.

LENA (to herself): Make yourself at home.

Lena crosses to the kitchen and sees the cooler door open and closes it. She shakes her head as she goes to the sink and washes pans. Julie moves things around, then suddenly spots Jimmy. As she lets out a scream and darts out of there, she knocks a pan of roast beef gravy over Jimmy. Lena freezes. Julie darts screaming from the cooler, followed by a screaming Lena to the front door. Julie runs out. Lena stops at the front door. Everyone hears Julie and Lena. Dawn gets a pack of playing cards from her purse and shuffles them. Terral looks at her as he and Lennox cross to the dining area. Charlie motions for Jolly to follow him. They cross to a door and exit. Moments later they enter the kitchen from a side door and rush into the cooler. Terral and Lennox are at the front door with Lena.

TERRAL: Who was that?

LENA: That's the director of a cruise line.

LENNOX: What was she screaming about?

LENA: She's overworked. Poor thing. That girl is working so hard to make this celebrity cruise line thing work.

Charlie and Jolly drag Jimmy out the cooler, he has gravy all over him.

LENNOX: We heard two screams.

LENA: I'm a sympathy screamer. You scream, I'm just gonna scream. It freaks me out.

Terral and Lennox look around outside for Julie. Charlie and Jolly look around for where to stash Jimmy. Charlie spots the flour bin. They drag Jimmy to it. Charlie opens it and they put him in it. Flour comes up out the bin like dust and settles on them. As they close the bin and push it back in place, Charlie spots the gravy on the floor.

JOLLY: Blood?

CHARLIE: Gravy. They might think it's blood.

Terral and Lennox enter the restaurant. Tas stands with Lena by the front door as they look for Julie. Charlie and Jolly frantically wipe up the gravy on the floor and flour bin, then exit through the side door.

LENNOX (to Lena): Where was she at when she screamed?

LENA: In the cooler.

Terral and Lennox enter the kitchen followed by Tas and Lena. They cross to the cooler when Lennox spots something on the floor. Charlie and Jolly enter through the side door and cross to the cast who pretend to be playing cards. They notice the cast looks at their clothes. Charlie and Jolly notice flour on their clothing. When they dust it off they notice it's on the floor. In the kitchen Lennox bends down to look at the several reddish-brown drops on the floor.

LENNOX: Blood.

Charlie whips off his shirt, leaving just his under shirt on. Charlie wipes up the floor, then throws the shirt to Jolly.

CHARLIE: Make sure I got everything, then get rid of it.

As Charlie crosses to the dining room door he notices the cast looks at him. Terral, cautiously inspects the drops. Lena and Tas watch them. Lena bends down with them.

LENNOX (to Lena): Watch out. Don't contaminate the evidence.

One member of the cast, after the other, give Charlie the "okay". He smiles as he walks into the dining area.

GARY: You doing it, Charlie!

Lena looks at Tas, who shrugs. Lena then sticks her finger in the drop and taste it, before the astounded cops can stop her.

LENA: Gravy.

Charlie looks around for them, as he spots something across the street. He crosses to the bar as he pretends not to have noticed. He pretends to look for something behind the bar, as he spies across the street. Julie makes her way closer and closer to the restaurant. Terral and Lennox look at the gravy on the floor. Tas and Lena see it.

LENA: NOW, I know why she was screamin'! She knows I'm gonna kill her, pourin' gravy on my floor!

Lena organizes her mop and bucket, the whole time complaining to herself. Tas walks to the dining room door followed by Terral and Lennox. Charlie rushes up to Jolly and the cast.

CHARLIE (to Jolly): Julie's coming back! The cops are gonna see her and she's gonna talk! I'm gonna try and stop her!! You.... get him out the flour bin and get rid of him!!

Charlie rushes out to dining area. Terral and Lennox make their way to the front door.

CHARLIE: Where ya'll been at?

They all look at Charlie in his undershirt. Jolly and the cast exit the side door and enter through the side door of the kitchen and pull Jimmy out of the flour bin. Lena, unaware of them, is partially seen as she mops the cooler floor.

LENA (O.S.) (to herself): She don't even ATTEMPT to wipe it up!

They carry Jimmy through the door and close it then enter the private dining area and close that door behind them, but a trail of flour was left all the way.

LENA (O.S.) (to herself): Wait a minute! Charlie said, don't go in the cooler. Did she see---

Lena is frozen.

LENA (cont'd): James Cain, are you in here?

Lena cautiously backs out of the cooler. Charlie crosses to the bar, as he tries to keep the police's attention. The cast seat Jimmie at the table with them.

CHARLIE: Ya'll haven't seen her either.

Everyone motions "no".

CHARLIE (cont'd): I'm beginning to think she's unstable.

TERRAL: Something's going on here. You ain't gonna tell me somethin' ain't going on here!

The cast place a cap and sun glasses on Jimmie. Jolly sees flour on him, then spots flour around on the floor. Jolly takes off his shirt leaving himself in his undershirt. He then dusts off Jimmy and the floor.

CHARLIE (to Police): I think she drinks.

LENNOX: Something's going on more then drinking.

Lena backs in from kitchen, keeping her focus on the kitchen door. John and Fred are walking to the restaurant. John watches Fred and Julie look at each other.

JOHN (to Fred): How'd you know I was coming here?

Tas and Lennox spot John and Fred. Tas lights up. Charlie's focused on Julie. Lena crosses to Tas.

TERRAL (to Charlie): Don't mess with the police.

Terral spots John.

JOHN: How'd you know I was going to be at the airport?

Dawn tries to deal playing cards but is distracted by Gary and Abe as they try to keep Jimmy sitting up. Jolly dusts the last of the flour he sees.

ABE (to Gary): Just stand next to him and hold him back by his shirt.

Jimmy falls face first onto table.

GARY: Being that you are his relative. Wouldn't it be a little more natural for you to be hanging out with him. ---Or is it perhaps that I am not as TALL....

ABE (sigh): I thought you were gonna say it's a....

Gary pulls Jimmy back in his chair.

GARY: Spit it out. Black thing!? I thought maybe you couldn't do it because....

ABE: --You got something on ya chest get it off! You gonna say something about I'm TOO OLD?!

JAMES: --Hey boy, watch the old stuff.

DAWN: I'm trying to deal here!

Jimmy falls again.

RUSSELL: Oi ve--y.

John smiles as he sees Tas through the door.

FRED (cont'd) (to John): Because we're connected. I am you and you are me.

JOHN: And we are all together.

FRED: Now ya gettin' it fatboy.

John tries to ignore Fred as they enter. Tas hurries to John, they are happy to see each other. Charlie notices Terral and Lennox are preoccupied with someone coming in. Charlie doesn't even see John, who is a little surprised.

JOHN: Hey.

TAS: What are you doin'.... Man, it's good.... You picked a strange time to show up.

John and the police acknowledge each other.

JOHN: How you guys doin?

Charlie steps outside past Fred. Tas sees John is surprised at Charlie not acknowledging him. Lena sees John.

TAS: We have a little problem.

LENNOX: How you doing Mister Woodman.

TERRAL (to John): Hey.

Charlie glances back in to see if he can cross to Julie. That's when he spots John. Julie sees the police and crosses to them. Charlie tries to stop her. She walks back in the restaurant followed by Charlie, who surrenders.

JULIE (to Terral and Lennox): Did you find Mr. James Cain?

JOHN (to Charlie): James Cain?

CHARLIE (to John): What are you doing here?

TERRAL (to Julie): Where is Mr. James Cain?

JULIE: He was hanging in that big refrigerator. Dead.

Lena's focus is taken completely away from John and turned to Julie.

LENNOX: The walk in refrigerator? We never went in there.

Julie urges Terral and Lennox to the kitchen.

TERRAL (to John): We'll talk to you after....

John motions okay to the police as they follow Julie into kitchen.

JOHN: What's going on, Charlie?

Fred crosses to the private dining area.

FRED: The ol' shell game, with a very large peanut.

TAS: Charlie's got this Rat Pack thing going with these old TV actors.

CHARLIE: Abe Goda hit his nephew James Cain on the head and killed him.

Lena covers her ears and hums to herself not wanting to hear anymore. John, notices her.

TAS (to John, about Lena): She can't be involved with any other murders.

Julie motions to the cooler. Lennox opens the door to the cooler. Julie waits for him to stick his head in. Fred walks up to cast table.

JULIE: He's hanging in the back left corner.

Julie looks in. Fred looks at Jimmy. The cast look at Fred as Dawn pretends to keep the card game going.

ABE (to Fred): What you think?

FRED: You understand in the joint, cigarettes are used for money.

John still looks at Lena, he turns to Charlie.

JOHN: Abe Goda is James Cain's uncle?

TAS: Did you catch the dead part?

John motions "yes".

Terral and Lennox are in the cooler with Julie, who looks around.

TERRAL (to Julie): You sure it's this cooler?

JULIE: I know what I saw.

Julie storms out of the cooler.

TAS (to John): Of all the times to come around here.... What are you....?

JOHN: I saw you guys on TV. "Expose." The oyster bit was great.

Julie enters from the kitchen followed by Terral and Lennox.

JULIE (to Charlie): Where's....?

Julie looks at the door to the private dining area. She then crosses to it and looks in. She shakes her head to herself, then looks back at Terral and Lennox.

JULIE (cont'd) (to Police): Well....

Terral and Lennox cross to Julie and follow her into the private dining area. Charlie, reluctantly, follows them. Behind him John, then Tas followed by Lena, who won't let her get far from her.

JOHN: Charlie, I gotta say something before I chicken-out.

As the cast pretend to play cards, Fred stands back with Jolly in his undershirt. Terral looks at Jolly. Charlie sneaks glances around for Jimmy, as Fred tries to inconspicuously point him out.

JOHN (cont'd) (to Charlie): Remember when we were kids, and we did "Streetcar"?

CHARLIE: No, remember when YOU did....

Charlie suddenly sees Jimmy.

CHARLIE (cont'd): "Streetcar".

Lennox crosses to Jimmy. Gary takes his hand off of Jimmy, who then falls face first on the table, stopping the game.

DAWN (to others): Narcolepsy. It's to you, James.

Jimmy moans, then sits up immediately and grabs his head. The cast is startled as Gary lets out a girlish scream, causing Lena and Julie to scream.

JIMMY (looking at the cast): What, I died and went to B actor heaven?

JAMES: HEY, boy!

ABE (to Jimmy): Apparently I didn't hit ya hard enough with that chair.

TERRAL: What's he talking about?

TAS (to Terral and Lennox): Abe, freaked out and hit his nephew, James Cain, in the head with a chair.

Jimmy looks at Abe who shrugs.

LENNOX (to Jimmy): I didn't know Abe Goda was your uncle.

JIMMY (still rubbing his head): Some things are better left unsaid.

ABE: You didn't say that when I got you that role in "The Godfather".

JIMMY: Here we go again.

When Jimmy lowers his head he feels his missing eyebrow and makes a painful grimace. Terral and Lennox look at his missing eyebrow.

LENNOX: So what's up with the missing eyebrow?

Jimmy compares eyebrows.

DAWN (to Gary): You couldn't just keep ya grip on him.

JIMMY: No wonder that's sore.

Charlie glances at his finger that still has some of the eyebrow hair on it. Jimmy looks at his reflection in the napkin holder. Charlie catches Jolly's look. Charlie holds his finger with the hair on it up.

JIMMY: What's all this-- Powder, on me?

Jimmy sees his hair on Charlie's finger.

JIMMY (cont'd): ---Is that mine!?

GARY (to Dawn): Why didn't you stand behind him and hold him!?

CHARLIE: Yeah, and that's flour.

TAS (to Jimmy): They thought he killed you. They were shuffling you around tryin' to hide you.

DAWN (to Gary): If I did I sure wouldn't have let him go!

JIMMY (to Abe): You tried to kill me?

ABE: You got in the way of the chair.

FRED: Just like in "The Godfather".

JIMMY: My character didn't die like that in "The Godfather". Where you been? Who's this guy?

GARY (to Dawn): What are you trying to say?

FRED: It should have. After that movie about the rabbits.

JIMMY: Hey! Everybody makes mistakes!

DAWN (to Gary): I think I just said it.

FRED: Not you. You've been a hundred percent wrong every time. Maybe you shoulda listened more to the ol' man.

Gary looks around. He sees Lena, who eggs him on.

ABE: I told him to do "Cuckoo's Nest". Instead he chose to roll around a skating rink with a big steel marble!

FRED (to Jimmy): I'd like to take you to the track and bet just the opposite.

JIMMY: This is coming from a man who co-stars with larva!?

GARY (to Dawn): You don't wanna mess with me!

FRED: It was worms. And it's not larva, it's larvae.

LENA: Tell her Gary!

John shakes it off as if he was hit.

JOHN (to Jimmy as he motions to Fred): You can see him?

JIMMY (to John): Of course I can see him. What, did you get hit in the head with a chair too?!

Terral and Lennox look at one another.

JOHN: Charlie. I brought the cookies to the rehearsal of "Streetcar". I crushed up peanuts.

CHARLIE (in shock, to John): You?

JOHN (embarrassed): I really didn't want the part. I wanted to act opposite Tas. I wanted to be in your place. My life should have been yours, Charlie.

JIMMY: I thought we were concentrating on me here.

Charlie threateningly holds his finger up with part of Jimmy's eyebrow on it. Jimmy surrenders.

CHARLIE (to John): I always felt that too. --But, if I hadn't of ended up here....

Charlie motions around.

CHARLIE (cont'd): I mean, I am in the middle of this, but I wouldn't have....

Charlie looks at Tas as they cross to each other.

TAS: Me?

JIMMY: Exactly. Which is where we are. Which is where we're supposed to be.

FRED (to Jimmy): Hey! You doin' me?

JIMMY (to Fred): I hope not. Because it made sense to me, and it scares me.

JOHN (to Jimmy): You can see him.

JIMMY: I wish I couldn't see any of you.

CHARLIE (to Tas): I know I haven't been showing it.

JOHN (to Fred): You ain't in my head?

FRED: I'm not that cerebral.

TAS: Charlie, you been showing me in your dumb awkward way. It just wasn't what I wanted to see.

CHARLIE: No, Tas, I've been reaching my whole life for something I thought I missed. When the whole time I was missing something I had. I think I'm old enough for children now.

JIMMY: Before I die, will someone tell me what happened?

ABE (to Jimmy): Hey, ya using my lines?

JIMMY (to Abe): The last thing I remember, I'm in Antonio's eating.... You and Gilligan's Island come in....

JAMES: Hey!

JIMMY: Yeah, you wanted me to eat over....(looks around) Here?

CHARLIE (to Jimmy): Excuse me?

ABE: You were stubborn even as a kid! That's why I hit you on your head! I should used a brick. I thought I killed you! You didn't have no pulse.

JIMMY: Ohhhhhh. The medicine I've been taking drops my blood pressure. --So, you brought me over here ripped off my eyebrow, dipped me in flour. What were you going to do next, fry me?

Terral grabs Abe to arrest him.

JIMMY (cont'd) (to Terral): Wait. Officer, you can't arrest him. My mother would never forgive me. He's old. Going a little senile--

ABE: Hey!

TERRAL (to Jimmy): We have a murder attempt here.

LENNOX: Yeah, no matter how we feel about it.

John motions for the Policemen to walk away from the others.

JOHN: Look guys, I'm planning on opening up a joint here in town, and I'm gonna need somebody to set-up the security thing for me. --But if this happens here.... with the bad publicity I couldn't possibly....

TERRAL: I here ya. This ain't no bribe? As long as this ain't no bribe.

JOHN: This ain't a bribe it's a fact.

Terral and Lennox look at one another.

ABE: What? Are we still doing 'Mamet' here?

GARY (to Abe): No.

LENNOX (to John as he motions to Jimmy): If he wants to forget about it--

GARY: Does this look like 'Mamet'?

TERRAL (to John): As long as everybody agrees, it's cool with me.

John turns to everyone who motions go ahead.

JOHN (to Policemen): Everything is cool?

Terral and Lennox nod agreeing. They head for the door. Tas sees Charlie shaking his head to himself.

JOHN (to Policemen): You guys got a card so I can get in touch when I put this together.

Terral gets a card out for John as they exit to dining area.

TAS (to Charlie): What?

CHARLIE: Nothing.

GARY (to Dawn): I'm sorry I was getting stressed out.

Charlie sees Tas looking at him.

DAWN (to Gary): Me too. I shouldn't have called you ah--....

CHARLIE: It's like he comes in and.... I'm running around like a maniac with this dead guy.

LENA (to Dawn): You right, girl. That ain't the ol' "Mary Ann" I know.

JIMMY (to Charlie): Ah, excuse me, I wasn't dead.

CHARLIE: That's right and he wasn't even dead.

JIMMY: And don't leave out ripping off eyebrows.

JOLLY (to Jimmy): He did try to draw them in with a marker first.

Jimmy looks at himself in the napkin holder again, closing one eye at a time.

John enters from dining area. Jimmie's shaking his head about his eyes.

FRED (to Jimmy): I told him it wouldn't work.

JOHN (to Fred): What are you doing here?

FRED: I'm here for you and Charlie.

CHARLIE: How are you here for me?

FRED: Charlie, you did what Shakespeare said about true love. It was love that was never consummated. That's what you did with acting. You gave the best performance I've ever seen on stage. ---And no one else saw it.

CHARLIE: You didn't see it?

FRED: That's what I mean. You did a James Dean number. You walked away. It was between that and one day sitting on a set in the desert waiting for some worm to come get me that I knew I was a hack.

DAWN: What is this guy talking about?

FRED: Sure, I had some good roles--

ABE: I don't think he knows.

JAMES: Aye.

FRED: --but the Fred Ward character wasn't working for me. That's when I adopted Bogart's persona, per se. I go back to Fred Ward when I have to act.

JIMMY: Has this guy always been like this? (To Abe) Or, did you hit him in the head too?!

ABE (to Jimmy): You little.... You see, you almost made me curse. You're the only one that needed it, you still need it!

JOHN (to Fred): You gonna be here until I make this right, huh? (To Charlie) Charlie, this is the idea I got.

Lights bump out.

SCENE 6

Charlie's new restaurant and dinner theater. Lights fade up on two dinner tables DSR. Antonio serves Jimmy as Abe waits on Tas and Charlie and their adopted 6 year old boy and 8 year old girl. At the next table a CUSTOMER and

WIFE glance at Jimmy's dish. Tas notices Abe is their waiter.

ABE (to Tas): I'm on probation.

JIMMY (low voice): Antonio, you make my life tolerable.

ANTONIO: Mr. Cain, it's my pleasure to serve you wherever you go.

CUSTOMER (to his wife): We didn't have to get this we coulda got that?

Jimmy and Abe quickly glance at the customer.

ABE (to Jimmy): Is he doing me?

Jimmy shrugs to Abe, who walks away. A WAITER walks up with a bottle of wine to Abe. Who motions to the customer for him.

ABE (to himself): The customers are doing me and I'm waiting tables.

Lights come up on a theater stage DSL, Gary is playing Stanley to Lena's, Stella, in "STREETCAR". Gary breaks away from Fred, James, and Russell's hold on him and runs after Lena who runs offstage. The waiter tries to open the bottle of wine for the customer.

JAMES (to Fred): Let him go.

LENA (O.S.) (crying): NO, NO, NO!!

Gary stops at the foot of the stairs.

GARY: Stel--

LENA (O.S.): I'll never come back, never!

Fred sees something in the audience. Fred leaves the stage, as James and Russell, shocked by this, pretend it isn't happening by focusing on Lena and Gary.

GARY: STELLA!

The waiter can't get the bottle of wine open. Fred surprises him and the customers he waits on by taking the bottle from him and looks at it then tries to open it.

FRED (to waiter): This year Merlot, gave everyone trouble.

Antonio finishes serving Jimmy.

GARY: Baby!

JIMMY (to Antonio as he motions to Fred): I love dinner theater.

THE END.

Interview with Magdalena Ball

Conducted by M. Stefan Strozier

Q: You are the author a new book of poems, *Quark Soup*, the self-help title, *The Art of Assessment*; and, most recently, the soon-to-be-published book, *Sleep Before Evening*. You also founded, and run, Compulsive Reader (www.compulsivereader.com). Given this wide breadth of genres and literary activities, how do you define yourself as a writer? And, along those lines, how important do you feel it is for a writer to define him or herself?

A: I'm certainly what you might call a jill-of-all-trades. I do think that the skills that make for a good writer of any particularly genre aren't different from those that make for a good writer in general. There's a common purpose in everything I write as it's all about creating/shaping/sharing meaning. I think if I had to order my activities in some kind of prioritized list of importance, the novels and poetry would precede the nonfiction, including the reviewing, but I like the balance of being able to move between genres and relieve the intense activity with lighter work.

In some ways it probably is important for a writer to have a certain milieu, if only to filter the great number of potential work into a smaller number of achievable goals. It also probably helps readers and publishers to present you in a way which can be categorized; however, I would hate to close any door that might have something interesting behind it. And of course I'm constantly breaking that rule. Having said that, there are certain types of writing that I'll probably never do – simply because I can't see myself successful at it – romance, comic novels, chick lit…(those words will probably come back to haunt me one day).

Q: Please describe your new book, *Sleep Before Evening,* and give us the story of how it came about.

A: *Sleep Before Evening* is the story of Marianne, a seventeen year old musical and academic prodigy who is on the brink of adulthood. Her grandfather, a famous philosopher, dies during a chess game with her, and his loss creates a vacuum in her life which ultimately leads her into the dangerous world of a hip harmonica player whose dissolute world challenges her preconceptions about art and life. There's plenty of anarchic squalor, music, poetry, substance abuse, sex and above all, the challenge of freedom which changes Marianne's self-definition. As you can tell, it's a coming of age story, mainly set in Manhattan's mean streets (which I was rather missing while I wrote).

I started writing while pregnant with my first child --stimulated no doubt by the creative hormones that come with pregnancy and the misconception that I would have lots of extra time to knock out a novel during my maternity leave! The novel took me about 6 years (my son is now 9!) between starting and completing the first draft and another 3 years of rewriting until it was ready for publication so it was a long gestation!

Q: Edgar Allen Poe was both a critic and a poet (he even wonderfully criticized his own work, such as *The Raven*). Similarly, George Bernard Shaw was a great critic of theater long before he tried to be a playwright. Conversely, there have been poets who were wonderful critics but lousy poets, such as Ezra Pound. There have also been wonderful critics who were poor prose writers, such as James Wood. Do you have any special insights into what it takes to be a good critic and a good poet (or writer, playwright, etc.) at the same time? Is there some balance that must be struck? Or, are the two things entirely unrelated?

A: I do think that there are insights into the creative process that only come with actually participating in it. Of course there is a balance and to write well you have to be able to turn the critic off in the first instance, while the critic can't be too sentimental to the difficulties encountered by a writer. I do always feel bad when I write a negative review—much worse than a critic who had no idea of the work involved in writing a novel would, but I don't let it stop me from casting a judgmental eye when it is warranted (though I have to say I don't write negative reviews lightly). I don't entirely dislike Pound's poetry, but I almost think that there is an inverse relationship between the role of the editor (which is actually quite different from the role of the critic), and the role of the writer, though perhaps both have (or should have) the same goal, which is a perfectly polished piece of fully realized world. Nevertheless, I read quite a lot of reviews and the best reviews are written by great writers (I'm thinking for example of Salman Rushdie's reviews, or those of Delia Falconer, both writers whose work as critics I admire almost as much as their work as novelists). Good writers are good readers and a good reviewer *must* be a good reader first and foremost, so there is most certainly a connection.

Q: As a critic whose career has spanned many years, have you noticed any particular trends with writers? For example, what types of works succeed and what types fail, in your assessment?

A: "Success" and "Failure" are relative terms and I imagine that my definition of what is a successful book might differ from a publishers! I haven't noticed any trends in literary fiction, which is what I read most often. Great books with classic innovative themes continue to be produced on such a wide and un-trendy range of themes that it is impossible to point to a trend. However, what I have noticed is that publishers in the main (particularly the large ones) tend to be less open to taking on new fiction and that there seems to be a hunger from purchasers for "reality" nonfiction – that is easy to ready and sensationalized "true-life" stories, which therefore puts pressure on memoirists to embellish their memoirs (à la James Frey). There also seems to be a trend for adults to buy young adult fiction as there is a perception that it's easier, lighter and more engaging. I believe however (and I've been very fortunate to have experienced it) that many smaller publishers tend to ignore these trends and to focus solely on quality over *trendiness*, which is probably a good thing, since trends change quickly and it's not safe to follow them.

Q: How do you write, and how are your writing techniques different – if at all – from when you write poetry vs. prose?

A: Poetry is a much less discursive activity for me than prose. I tend to write it based on a broad concept and overriding emotion, and build the poem immediately from scratch around that. Fiction on the other hand involves plotting and a very discursive progress so I tend to build a frame first (eg outline, plot points, character profiles, chapter concepts) and then begin writing onto the frame (which will invariably change but nonetheless keeps the writing focused). Poetry is a much easier and more instantly satisfying process for me. Fiction takes a lot of craftwork before I can let instinct take over and is therefore much slower for me.

Q: What is your opinion of the present state of poetry?

A: I'm very lucky in that, between Compulsive Reader and Thylazine (where I'm poetry reviews editor), I get to read quite a lot of modern poetry. I have to say that I'm very excited about the present state of poetry. There is so much wonderful, utterly relevant, powerful work coming out which is totally readable, pithy, beautiful, and absolutely groundbreaking. I do have more access to Australian poetry, so my experiences may be skewed, but I think that people are actually starting to purchase poetry and to expect it to be as pleasurable an experience for them as any other form of reading. The notion of poetry being a hi-brow or solely academic and painful pursuit is long gone. I also love the way poetry is expanding into film (I'm thinking for example of Dorothy Porter's Monkey Mask), multimedia, novels in verse and theatre. I've always found experimentalism for its own sake to be unpleasant and have never been a big fan of the "post-modern" school of poetry, but I don't come across it often. What I do see is a lot of great modern poets like Les Murray, Dorothy Porter, Luke Davies and Mike Ladd, who are making full use of the media and creating meaning which is perfectly relevant for the modern reader.

Q: What has worked for you, as a professional writer, in terms of a successful career, and what has not worked for you? And, what advice would you give to emerging writers?

A: I'll give the advice first, which is to turn the critic off while writing. I spent many fallow years (from a writing perspective) ignoring the muse because I was too worried that my work couldn't meet my own exacting standards. If you want to write you simply have to put the words on the page – it's as easy as that, at least in the first instance. You only learn and grow as a writer by continuing to work through the doubt and fear, and you can only polish and edit *after* there is something to polish or edit.

For me, I've got a zillion conflicting priorities and writing, especially the big stuff like novels, always feels like a bit of indulgence where there are mouths to feed and urgent demands for nonfiction work. I rely on planning. I simply have to put down an annual, monthly, weekly and daily plan for what I'm going to do and schedule in the big stuff so it has the same imperative as the little stuff. Otherwise it would continually go to the bottom of the list. The other thing is to get a writing partner and push one another. Again, this is particularly critical for big long term projects like a novel – I set myself a deadline and so does my partner and we then feel the pressure of that deadline, knowing that there is a reader eager to receive our work.

Q: What are your thoughts and feelings about the rise of the Internet as a publishing medium, and the effect it has had on established traditions of print publishing?

A: I'm a huge fan of the Internet. I feel it has leveled the playing field between the big publishers and small ones, and I love the way it unites on a worldwide basis, a community of like-minded people. This flows through to publishing, since I feel, in my little mountain home in Australia, that I can reach a readership all over the world—in big cities or small towns. I also feel that my small publisher now has the same promotional power as the big 5 which is, in some ways, revolutionary. That said, the ease of publishing on the Internet, and the way work can be made to "look" great with little effort, means that good editing is more critical than ever before (and paradoxically, less used than ever before) so there is a mass of poorly editing work reaching the public before it is ready. There is so much work involved in taking a concept to a fully publishable novel (the editing is almost everything – inspiration is only about 10% of the work involved), and the ease of publishing makes it tempting to take shortcuts. The result is an overabundance of junk. So, my answer is, I love the Internet, but it's no substitution for the aspects of writing which will never change – hard work and excellent editors. I still believe fairly strongly in that funnel.

Q: What are your plans for the future?

A: My immediate plans are all about promoting (through performance) my poetry book *Quark Soup* and novel *Sleep Before Evening* but I'm in the process of partnering with someone to push me towards completing my next novel which is about a scientist in search for a theory of everything.

I've also got a ton of little collaborations in multimedia work, with a new poetry/painting book, and a biography. I rarely say no to anything interesting sounding, so the door is still wide open!

Media, Ethics, and War

by Ernest Dempsey

It would be redundant to argue for the role of the media of information in our life today. Though residing in our houses, we actually live in the world through print media, radio, TV, and more recently, the Internet. The world is a global community because we see the way men are, and they way they live, think, and act. All this information comes to us through the media. From a psychological point of view, man's self-concept is built to a large degree by his understanding of himself. If the human child thinks he is a peaceful and benevolent thing, he tends to act like that in his adult life. His choices are peaceful and his thinking is directed toward benevolent action. We, and our children, are immersed in the deluge of media in the present day world of information and services. Hence, it can be asserted with confidence that news, views, and other programs coming from radio, television, newspapers and magazines, and the Internet build a large part of our self-concept. It becomes a matter of importance then to see whether our self-concept in development, coming from the global media, is a constructive one or the contrary.

As these media take us out of our habitat, ethical questions take a rise from various sides. Most of these questions protest the effects of media upon a particular culture or a part of it. This is akin to defensive measures of one group of men against the invasion of another group with notable differences, especially of culture. Media is the weapon used to proselytize the foe, or, in times of a more open and aggressive conflict, demoralize the enemy and glorify the cause of the war. In this sense, media serves as something advantageous to one human group and disastrous to a hostile one. However, there is a deeper and more serious sense in which media has been, and is, undermining the whole of the human sentience and reason. This sense relates to war situations and the role of media in such times to present them before men. And it is in this sense that I contend to make my point about the silent holocaust of our humanness at the hands of our ever-expanding media.

Although we come across such books as 'Societies at Peace' (Signe Howell and Roy Willis, 1989) that contend for a peaceful intrinsic nature of man, in most part of our known world man does seem to possess cruel impulses (whether intrinsic or acquired is another matter). Men are grouped and groups fight for domination. Tools used to strengthen the feelings of belongingness to a group, and of hostility to other, are well-known and well-discussed now: religion, race, language, nationality, and ideology mainly, not to mention many other. All these contribute, solely or in varying degrees, to start a war, the main motive for which now a days, if hasn't always been, is economic self-interest. With the outset of war, the role of all these agencies practically ceases as that of a match after the kindling of fire. War propels itself almost automatically towards the desired state depending on the relative strength of the conflicting groups. The role of media, however, is more pervasive and lasting. During the time when war is being cooked up, media remains the regulating knob of the burner. News bulletins, interviews, special reports, speeches of leaders, all make the mind of the listener, or reader, to expect war as the outcome of the prevailing controversy. The leaders of both sides make valorous determinations with the impression that *they* are not afraid of the enemy and that they are the *right* side. The layman sees them, reads them, and hears them, soon forgetting his rational fear of the *expected* war of which he couldn't formerly sleep well. Since the newspapers, TV, radio, and the Internet of his side all assure him of his strength; he soon forgets that leaders and men of media have their funk holes ready to save them while he is the direct target of the pendent disaster. Media makes the war interesting and even attractive by presenting the conflict in a curious way. While telling of war, newscasters are shown quite calm and disinterested with no sign of worry or fear, or even of the least concern. Voices on radio bulletins and shows are as fearless as ever; newspapers and websites always show the comments on tense situations in the third person, of presidents, prime ministers, defense ministers, officials, analysts, and others. It sounds as if the editorial staff is quite disinterested and unconcerned. Media makes war a theatrical presentation to observe and, preferably, enjoy. War is initiated and it is then that the more dehumanizing role of media takes over. As long as the war lasts, the reckless outcome, the corpses, the wounded, the affected, the victims, and all the destruction of the cultural products are informed of in such a curious, episodic manner that the audience soon gets addicted to this sensation. The recent wars in Afghanistan and Iraq are the classic examples of the abuse of Media at the hands of those who earn from it. By beginning every bulletin with news of casualties and destruction in war, media offers tempting bait to the frustrated and repressed part of our nature that is always dying to have an enemy and its obliteration. We are given the feeling that we must observe the real-life *Mortal Kombat* and choose our side. An interesting tool to raise the curiosity of the audience is putting correspondents on who are reporting directly from the battle place. This is an outrageous act since it is only meant to observe the war more closely through another person's participation in the war experience and that person is as fearless and impartial as anyone possibly can be. One wonders whether the newscaster's voice is not enough to inform us of the situation. But how could the situation be that exciting? Media serves as the *saucy ketchup* with the *hot fries*. Beyond all this vicious temptation of the war situation, media undoubtedly seeks its economic self-interest. The paper or channel that presents the war in the most thrilling way sells most and hence earns most. It is interesting to observe how after such violent wars as these of Iraq and Afghanistan, the newsmakers revert to the old conflicts of Kashmir and Palestine so that war in media always holds the first place. The war continues and so do its pleasures that media blesses us with.

Through social psychology, we know of the looking-glass self, part of the self that is constituted or adjusted by taking someone else's view of the social world and our place in it. Hence no detailed account of the concept except that we know by now its pivotal role in our self-concept, the way we see ourselves. It is congruent to the way we see ourselves through the eyes of the others. And we feel to do what we see we are and what we can do, or more precisely, what we are mean to do. I see horrors taking over a sensible and compassionate being who comes to see the role of the international looking-glass (that of the media) in our self-concept. With all the papers printing headlines of war, all magazines bearing title covers adorned with leaders of warring groups, all news bulletins starting with and centering on war news, there hardly remains anything of our self-concept except that we are meant for war. Never have I seen news bulletins that start with a cheerful piece of information of some creative or positive, peaceful act performed by an ordinary human being. There are people who write good books and articles, artists who portray great expressions, musicians who compose sweet melodies and countless others who do human and humane acts every passing day. How much time media takes to circulate the benevolence of such contributions in its daily schedule? Much less than it takes to show our filthiness. We are not shown writing but shooting, not singing but screaming and yelling, not loving but killing. Our media never realizes that in proliferating our own horrors it is not reforming our attitude by arising empathy but, more emphatically, teaching us that we are essentially destructive and hateful.

Media does not, and can not, remind us some lost lesson of humanity by spilling our own blood. It teaches us that we can spill blood and that many of us out there are doing it and that with pride. I shudder to think that some day in the near future there is going to be an ad on the screen in which a hitman, being shown to kill a citizen for his money, will laugh roguishly and say, 'Why not try this, folks!' This is exactly what our media is doing these days; persuading us that we are killing-machines and it's all right being so. By reminding us persistently that we are a killing species, media has caused and is still causing among us *Psychic Numbing*; we are rapidly getting habituated to the killing shown on our screens and talked of on our radio and in the print. So much so that we don't even take interest in news if war is not there. My aunt stopped listening to the radio as soon as the war in Iraq was over, complaining that there was nothing *special* in it now. Others I know had a more or less similar response. This provoked me to think critically over the role of media and our attitude. A thorough reflection on the matter brought me to the link between the way we are informed of ourselves and the way we feel to think and act. I strongly believe at this stage that the media must change its way of presentation of human situation if it has a concept of and care for good and bad. This brings us to media and morality, since media is teaching what to think and do, and morality seeks to check all that leads to harmful thinking and doing.

There seems to be nothing wrong with the presentation of media except the manner in which it does so. If it could be imparted only that all the bloody things before us are not fries with sauce but a deplorable situation felt strongly by those who sit behind the desk telling this, a major part of the unethical nature of such presentation would be resolved, though the development-of-self-concept dilemma would need a more thorough treatment. This would more effectively be dealt with by giving priority to constructive aspects of human nature/nurture. In the age of growing individualism when people are dependent to a great degree on means of information directly, the ethical responsibility of media is accentuated. Now when we are becoming the ancient infants of a modern mother, that is media, I strongly feel the revival of Plato's contention: Stories told to children should be carefully filtered, or more precisely, carefully arranged to present. Though we have been turned much into war-devouring species, there seems no reason why we shouldn't welcome the smiling human being in our media than the one with a gun. Self-concept can be altered and to my humble wisdom I don't see why such a benevolent presentation won't earn more than a bloody one. The inertia of our warring-species concept is not that strong as the media may suppose but stopping the unethical presentation of the devastating activities of ours will help put an end to much of the suffering and apathy that is prevalent among the masses at the hour. The great power of media can do more than it takes pride in. It only has to realize its right and wrong. Clearly it is a question of law then, to realize the impact of the streaming information with which the media deluges the man.

Nearly all the nations abstain from presenting porn in their news bulletins. The policies of the major channels and print sources seem to realize that things defined noxious in the culture should not be propagated unchecked. It is pitiable then not to see such a care in case of things known noxious in human knowledge. Destructive presentation of human potential is far more threatening than one imagines ordinarily. In teaching abnormal psychology, it is instructed beforehand not to label someone or oneself, unless thorough examination of the condition in question confirms a disorder. Letting the sources of the development of self-concept label the whole of humanity as destructive is an act of violation in itself. Only the lawmakers haven't realized it yet. While showing man killing and ravaging most of the time, and not saving and creating, the world media is playing the role of a fagin who is coaxing its viewers subtly into conflict and acts of violence. Given the psychological impact of such a role, and the ensuing behavioral consequences, it feels necessary to formulate a revised international law concerning the policies of the international media. Such a law should keep in view the role of media in shaping a person's overall attitude and self-concept. Hence, it should advocate a greater emphasis on presentation of man as a peaceful species of the planet that not only behaves benevolently towards its own kind but also takes care of other life forms on the planet. It should monitor the time given to news and features of violence and the way they are presented to the audience. Basing its clauses on the findings of behavioral sciences and other disciplines, such a law should prevent the distortion of the concept of human being as something meant to kill and destroy. And it must show man as a caring and responsible element of nature that can, and does, strive to make things better on earth. Artists, men of knowledge, responsible figures from all levels of life should be brought to surface and their efforts and achievements highlighted. This will help inspire the viewer to act magnanimously and not ignobly.

Certainly such an international law has to be one above economic self-interest. It must be directed toward peace. Its policy should be global so that local media is in accord with the broader flux of information. Sources of media who violate its policies should be challenged in the International Court of Justice and any necessary reforms should be sanctioned directly from the international community.

Contributors

Magdalena Ball runs The Compulsive Reader www.compulsivereader.com. Her stories, editorials, poetry, reviews and articles have appeared in a wide number of printed anthologies and journals, and have won many awards. She is the author of The Art of Assessment, and Quark Soup (available from http://www.compulsivereader.com/html/images/quarkindex.htm) Her novel Sleep Before Evening will be available from BeWrite Books early in 2007.

Edward L. Betz Jr. is from New Orleans, LA. His screenplays RENOVATORS, and a short version of ONLY HIS KNEES, were shot in New Orleans, and also by the Vancouver Film School. MARTA, another screenplay, won 2nd place in the Los Angeles Screenplay Competition. His play, CHARLIE'S OYSTER, won 1st place in a CAC competition, and his play, CURSES, won 2nd place in the same competition. CURSES won 1st place in the Deep South Writers Conference. A play version of ONLY HIS KNEES was produced in New Orleans, London, Edinburgh, and the American Repertory Theater. ONLY HIS KNEES and LOSIN MANNIE were produced by La Muse Venale Acting Troupe in November, 2005, at Where Eagles Dare Theater, NY, NY. His address is 70513 Fourth Street, Covington, LA 70433; PHONE: 985-871-9972; EMAIL: e_betz@lycos.com.

Abdul Karim Khan (pen name: Ernest Dempsey) was born in Hangu, a small town in Pakistan. As a child, he enjoyed two things: The joyful company of his brother and Khan's best friend, Shais; and, making airy castles with lots of characters in his mind. These two things pervaded through his spirit so much that he has given up valuable scholarships to pursue them. At twelve, he began his career by writing detective stories, horror, thrillers, and whatnot). However, a career in writing held no bright prospects in his society. So he studied geology. But his literary spirit demanded more attention and he started studying classics, alongside writing. The Internet reached his hometown in 2003, whereupon he began submitting his work to literary ezines. In just the last year, he has seen publication of his poems, essays, short stories, and literary reviews. He has been published in audience literary journal, and other literary journals, as well as other magazines. His reviews appear in The audience Review, and other places. Email: dempsey87@yahoo.com.

Michele Harvey is a substitute teacher living with her two sons in Denver, Colorado. Her first poetry chapbook, Ripped Railway Tickets was recently published by Enjambed Press. For inquiries please visit her website at: www.MicheleHarveycom.com. Michele's poetry has appeared in several literary journals including The Litchfield Review and Main Channel Voices.

Doug Holder is the founder of the Ibbetson Street Press of Somerville, Mass. His poetry and prose has appeared in "Presa," "The Café Review," "The Boston Globe," "the new renaissance," "Main Street Rag," "Poetry Motel," and many more. He holds an M.A. in English and American Literature and Language from Harvard University.

Harendran Kallinkeel resides in Taliparamba (Kerala) with his family and owns a farm of rubber, coconut, pepper and areca nuts. He helps US college students online, and owns a company: www.kallinkeelconsultancy.com/. He is published in literary print journals, and in numerous online ezines. *audience* is the brainchild of Harendran Kallinkeel and M. Stefan Strozier.

Mary C. O'Malley has an MFA in Creative Writing from Spalding University. She also has a LISW and has worked in the urban centers of Cleveland for over twenty years. She has five children including two sets of twins. She has been published in anthologies such as Cleveland in Prose and Poetry and Connections 2003.Her work has been included in several productions of the Greater Cleveland Poets and Writer's League and has been in The Mid America Poetry Review, Whiskey Island, Tributaries 6,7,8 and North Central Review. On the internet her work has been included in The Box Car Review, Cezanne's Carrots, Lunaristy, Poetry Midwest, Silk Road, Sage of Consciousness, and Big Pond Rumours.

Jean Russell lives in Burke, Virginia. Some of her stories have appeared in True Stories: Fiction by Uncommon Women (Red Dragon Press) and The Art of Life (Southwestern Publishing). Her poetry has appeared in many national literary journals, including Potomac Review and Poetic License in London. Jean is currently working on her play called "Petunia."

Lee Stringer lived on the streets from the early eighties until the mid—nineties. He the author of *Sleepaway School, Like Shaking Hands with God,* and *Grand Central Winter.* He is a former editor and columnist of *Street News*. His essays and articles have appeared in a variety of other publications, including The Nation, The New York Times, and Newsday. He lives in Mamaroneck, New York.

M. Stefan Strozier (www.mstefanstrozier.org) lives in New York City. He is the founder and artistic director of La Muse Venale Acting Troupe (www.lamusevenale.org). His plays, *Guns, Shackles & Winter Coats, The Whales,* and *The Tragedy of Abraham Lincoln* were performed in lengthy runs, off-off Broadway, and in the Midtown International Theatre Festival. He has directed four plays and produced ten, all off-off Broadway. His stories, poems, non-fiction have been published in literary online and print zines, and in magazines and newspapers.

Mel Waldman, Ph. D. is a licensed New York State psychologist and a candidate in Psychoanalysis at the Center for Modern Psychoanalytic

Studies (CMPS). He is also a poet, writer, artist, and singer/songwriter. After 9/11, he wrote 4 songs, including "Our Song," which addresses the tragedy. His stories have appeared in numerous literary reviews and commercial magazines including HAPPY, SWEET ANNIE PRESS, CHILDREN, CHURCHES AND DADDIES and DOWN IN THE DIRT (SCARS PUBLICATIONS), NEW THOUGHT JOURNAL, THE BROOKLYN LITERARY REVIEW, HARDBOILED, HARDBOILED DETECTIVE, DETECTIVE STORY MAGAZINE, ESPIONAGE, and THE SAINT. He is a past winner of the literary GRADIVA AWARD in Psychoanalysis and was nominated for a PUSHCART PRIZE in literature. Periodically, he has given poetry and prose readings and has appeared on national T.V. and cable T.V. He is a member of Mystery Writers of America, Private Eye Writers of America, American Mensa, Ltd., and the American Psychological Association. He is currently working on a mystery novel inspired by Freud's case studies. *Who Killed the Heartbreak Kid?*, a mystery novel, was published by iUniverse in February 2006. It can be purchased at www.iuniverse.com/bookstore/, www.bn.com, at www.amazon.com, and other online bookstores or through local bookstores. Recently, some of his poems have appeared online in THE JERUSALEM POST.

Matthew Ward (Newcastle, Australia) started writing seriously in 1993. In 1994, he had poetry published in OPUS (Newcastle University's magazine), Newcastle Herald, Writer's World, and JIGs (Journal of

Interdisciplinary & Gender Studies). He has written serious articles for literary newsletters, and satirical ones for the now defunct www.theLiberals.org. His short stories have appeared in OPUS. In 2004, his story *Jake With A Snarly Smile On His Chops* was published as a novella by Independence Jones (Australia). In 2006, he wrote two IT-related e-books. Matthew continues to write when he finds the time away from his web design business. It is only in this year, 2006, that he has started submitting his short stories to competitions. He has novels & screenplays 'in the works'. He is constantly trying to 'write outside the box', and this keeps him enthusiastic for the art that is creative writing. Matt is also the founder, owner, editor and publisher of Skive Magazine (www.skivemagazine.com).

Subscribe to *audience*!

Send your payment to: World Audience Publishers

25 Sickles Street, #6E

New York, NY 10040

Cell. (347) 226-0872; Ph. (347) 523-9727; Fax. (347) 523-9727

subscriptions@worldaudience.org

www.worldaudience.org

Subscribe now and save off the cover price ($11.99)!

☐ Please send one year (4 issues), $35.97

☐ Please send two years, $71.94

☐ Please send one current issue, $11.99

☐ Please send one back issue, no. ______, $11.99

☐ Please accept my donation, $______.

Make checks to: World Audience, Inc. Send my subscription to:

____

____

____

____

Submit your work:

submissions@worldaudience.org

World Audience, Inc.

www.worldaudience.org

La Muse Vénale Acting Troupe!

www.lamusevenale.org

Printed in the United States
65125LVS00007B/8

9 781934 209097